Current Chinese Economic Report Series

The Current Chinese Economic Reports series provides insights into the economic development of one of the largest and fastest growing economies in the world; though widely discussed internationally, many facets of its current development remain unknown to the English speaking world. All reports contain new data, which was previously unknown or unavailable outside of China. The series covers regional development, industry reports, as well as special topics like environmental or demographical issues.

More information about this series at http://www.springer.com/series/11028

Center for Macroeconomic Research at Xiamen
University
Editor

China's Macroeconomic Outlook

Quarterly Forecast and Analysis Report, March 2020

Springer

Center for Macroeconomic Research at
Xiamen University
Xiamen, Fujian, China

Grants: the major research projects of philosophy and social sciences of China's Ministry of Education of China (16JZD016), the key research projects of the Key Research Institutions of Humanities and Social Sciences at Universities (17JJD790014, 18JJD790007, 18JJD790008), the project of China National Social Science Foundation (17BJY086), the project of China Natural Science Foundation (71503222, 71740022).

ISSN 2194-7937 ISSN 2194-7945 (electronic)
Current Chinese Economic Report Series
ISBN 978-981-15-9278-2 ISBN 978-981-15-9279-9 (eBook)
https://doi.org/10.1007/978-981-15-9279-9

This Springer imprint is published by the registered company Springer Nature Singapore Pte Ltd.
The registered company address is: 152 Beach Road, #21-01/04 Gateway East, Singapore 189721, Singapore

Preface

This report is a partial result of the China's Quarterly Macroeconometric Model (CQMM), a project developed and maintained by the Center for Macroeconomic Research (CMR) at Xiamen University. The CMR is one of the Key Research Institutes of Humanities and Social Sciences sponsored by the Ministry of Education of China, focusing on Chinese economic growth and macroeconomic policies. The CMR started to develop the CQMM for purpose of short-term forecast, policy analysis, and simulation in 2005.

Based on the CQMM, the CMR with its partners hold press conferences to release forecasts for China' major macroeconomic variables. Since July 2006, twenty-six quarterly reports titled Chinese Macroeconomic Outlook have been presented and thirteen annual reports have been published. This 28th quarterly report was presented at the Forum on Chinese Macroeconomic Prospects and Press Conference of the CQMM at Xiamen University on March 31, 2020. This video conference was jointly held by Xiamen University and Economic Information Daily of Xinhua News Agency.

Xiamen, China

Center for Macroeconomic
Research at Xiamen University

Acknowledgements

Sorted by Chinese phonetic alphabet by name, 121 experts participated in the first questionnaire survey from January 20th–February 20th, 2020. Their names are: Bo Peiwen, Bi Jiyao, Chang Xin, Chen Changbing, Chen Gong, Chen Jianbao, Chen Jinmei, Chen langnan, Chen Lei, Chen Menggen, Chen Shoudong, Chen Xikang, Chen Xuebin, Chen Yanbin, Chen Zhiyong, Chen Yongjun, Dai kuisau, Deng Xiang, Dong ximiao, Dong Jichang, fan Ziying, Geng Qiang, Guo Qiyou Guo Xibao, Guo Xiaohe, Guo Zhiyi, Han Zhaozhou, he Jingtong, Hu Ridong, Hua Lecheng, Huang Xianfeng, Huang maoxing, Jian Jinhan, Jian Xinhua, Jiang yongmu, Jin Tao, Li Chen, Li Shi, Li Chunqi, Li Jianwei, Li Jun, Li Xuesong, Li Yingdong, Lin Xuegui, Liu Jianping, Liu Qianzhi, Liu Fengliang, Liu Xiaoxin, Liang Jiarui, Lai Desheng, L. V. Hanguang, Peng suling, pangmingchuan Qu wanwen, Ren Ruoen, Shao Yihang, Shen guobing, Shen Lisheng, Shi Junyi, Su Jian, sun Shaoyan, Sun Wei, Tang Jijun, Qin Wei, Wang Tongsan, Wang Changyun, Wang Dashu, Wang Guocheng, Wang Jiping, Wang Junbo, Wang Liyong, Wang Meijin, Wang Susheng, Wang Xi, Wang Yanxing, Wang Yuesheng, Wang Jinchao, Wang Jinbin, Wen Chuanhao, Wu Huabin, Wu Xinru, Wu kaichao, Xie Danyang Xie Di, Xie pan, Xin benjian, Xu Yifan, Xu Wenbin, Yan Ping, Yang Chengyu, Yang Cuihong, Yang Zhiyong, Yi Xianrong, Yin Xingmin, Yu Li, Yu Zuo, Yuan Fuhua, Yin Heng, Zang Xuheng, Zhang Donghui, Zhang Liqun, Zhang Liancheng, Zhang long, Zhang Mingzhi, Zhang Monan, Zhang Ping, Zhang Hongwei, Zhang Yuan, Zeng Wuyi, Zhi Dalin, Zhao Minghao, Zhao Xindong, Zhao Zhenquan, Zhao Zhijun, Zheng Chaoyu, zhouliqun, Zhoubing, zhouzejiong, Zhu Baohua, Zhu Jianping, Zhu Qigui.

The experts participating in the questionnaire are from the Department of macroeconomic research of the development research center of the State Council, the macro Research Institute of the national development and Reform Commission, the research center of prediction science of the Chinese Academy of Sciences, the Financial Research Institute of the Chinese Academy of Social Sciences, the economic Research Institute of the Chinese Academy of Social Sciences, the quantitative economic and Technological Economic Research Institute of the Chinese Academy of Social Sciences, and the Financial Strategy Research Institute of the

Chinese Academy of social sciences Research Institute, Research Institute of the Ministry of Commerce, National Bureau of statistics, external liaison department of the Central Committee of the Communist Party of China, China International Economic Exchange Center, internal participation Department of the people's daily, Hengfeng Bank Research Institute, contractor bank, China Banking Association, Central Party school, Taiwan "Chinese Academy of Sciences", "Chinese Academy of Sciences" Economic Research Institute, Chinese Academy of economics and other institutions, as well as Xiamen University and University of Chinese Academy of Sciences Shanghai University of international business and economics, Capital University of business and economics, Fujian Normal University, Liaoning University, Zhongshan University, Shandong University, Northeast University of Finance and economics, Northeast Normal University, Beijing Normal University, Beijing University of Aeronautics and Astronautics, Guangxi University, Jilin University, people's University of China, Zhongnan University of Finance and law, Zhejiang University of Finance and economics, Shanghai University of Finance and economics, Anhui University of Finance and economics Sichuan University, Peking University, Nanjing University, Nankai University, Shanghai University of Finance and economics, Wuhan University, East China Normal University, Jinan University, Lanzhou University, overseas Chinese University, Central University of Finance and economics, Xi'an Jiaotong University, Taiwan University, Northwest University, Southwest University of Finance and economics, Chongqing Business University, Shaanxi Normal University, Fudan University, Tianjin Business University, Tianjin University of Finance and Economics University of science and technology of Hong Kong, City University of Hong Kong, Lingnan University of Hong Kong, Shanghai Jiaotong University, etc.

Sorted by Chinese phonetic alphabet by name, 105 experts participated in the second questionnaire survey from March 18th to March 25th, 2020. Their names are: Bo Peiwen, Bi Jiyao, Chen Changbing, Chen Gong, Chen Jianbao, Chen Jinmei, Chen langnan, Chen Lei, Chen Menggen, Chen Shoudong, Chen Xikang, Chen Xuebin, Chen Yanbin, Chen Zhiyong, Chen Yongjun, Dai kuizao, Deng Xiang, Dong ximiao, Dong Jichang, Geng Qiang, Guo Qiyou, Guo Xibao, Guo Xiaohe Guo Zhiyi, Han Zhaozhou, he Jingtong, Hu Ridong, Hua Lecheng, Huang Xianfeng, Huang maoxing, Jian Jinhan, Jian Xinhua, Jiang yongmu, Jin Tao, Li Yi, Li Chunqi, Li Jianwei, Li Jun, Li Xuesong, Li Yingdong, Lin Xuegui, Liu Jianping, Liu Qianzhi, Liu Xiaoxin, Liang Jiarui, Lai Desheng, LV Hanguang, Qu wanwen, Ren Ruoen, Shao Yihang, Shen guobing, Shen Lisheng, Su Jian Sun Shaoyan, Sun Wei, Tang Jijun, Qin Wei, Wang Tongsan, Wang Changyun, Wang Dashu, Wang Guocheng, Wang Jiping, Wang Junbo, Wang Jinbin, Wang Liyong, Wang Meijin, Wang Susheng, Wang Yanxing, Wang Yuesheng, Wang Jinchao, Wen Chuanhao, Wu Huabin, Wu Xinru, Wu kaichao, Xie Danyang, Xie Di, Xie pan, Xin benjian, Xu Yifan, Xu Wenbin, Yan Ping, Yang Chengyu, Yang Cuihong Yi Xianrong, Yin Xingmin, Yu Li, Yu Zuo, Yuan Fuhua, Zang Xuheng, Zhang Donghui, Zhang Liqun, Zhang Mingzhi, Zhang Ping, Zhang Hongwei, Zhang Yuan, Zeng Wuyi, Zhao Minghao, Zhao Xindong, Zhao Zhenquan, Zheng Chaoyu, Zhou Liqun, Zhou zejiong, Zhu Baohua, Zhu Jianping, Zhu Qigui.

The experts participating in the questionnaire are from the Department of macroeconomic research of the development research center of the State Council, the macro Research Institute of the national development and Reform Commission, the research center of prediction science of the Chinese Academy of Sciences, the Financial Research Institute of the Chinese Academy of Social Sciences, the economic Research Institute of the Chinese Academy of Social Sciences, the quantitative economic and Technological Economic Research Institute of the Chinese Academy of Social Sciences, and the Financial Strategy Research Institute of the Chinese Academy of social sciences Research Institute, Research Institute of the Ministry of Commerce, National Bureau of statistics, Foreign Liaison Department of the CPC Central Committee, internal participation Department of the people's daily, Hengfeng Bank Research Institute, contractor bank, China Banking Association, Central Party school, Taiwan's "China Research Institute" and "China Research Institute" economic Research Institute, as well as Xiamen University, University of Chinese Academy of Sciences, Shanghai University of foreign trade and economic cooperation, Fujian Normal University, Liaoning Province University, Zhongshan University, Shandong University, Northeast University of Finance and economics, Beijing Normal University, Beijing University of Aeronautics and Astronautics, Guangxi University, Jilin University, Renmin University of China, Zhongnan University of Finance and law, Zhejiang University of Finance and economics, Shanghai University of Finance and economics, Anhui University of Finance and Economics, Sichuan University, Peking University, Nanjing University, Nankai University, Shanghai University of Finance and economics, Wuhan University, China East Normal University, Jinan University, Lanzhou University, overseas Chinese University, Central University of Finance and economics, Xi'an Jiaotong University, Taiwan University, Southwest University of Finance and economics, Chongqing Business University, Shaanxi Normal University, Fudan University, Tianjin Business University, Tianjin University of Finance and economics, Hong Kong University of science and technology, Hong Kong City University, Hong Kong Lingnan University, Shanghai Jiaotong University and other universities.

We would like to express our sincere gratitude to all of the above experts for their active participation and insights.

Principal Investigator

Min Gong

Members of Our Research Team

Zhiyuan Lin, Yanwu Wang, Huakun Wu, Changlin Yu, Guifu Chen, Weiteng Chin, Yanping Huang, Yu Liu, Shengrong Lu, Jing Li, Wenpu Li.

Executive Summary

In 2019, the weakening of global trade expansion restrained the growth of private investment in Chinese manufacturing industry; the continued strict implementation of policies to guard against financial risks restrained the growth of real estate investment and infrastructure investment. Slower investment became the main downward pressure on economic growth. Gross domestic product (GDP) grew by 6.1% in real terms in 2019, down 0.6 percentage points over the previous year. In order to cope with the downward pressure at home and from abroad, the Chinese government has strengthened and improved macro-control, introduced a series of policies and measures, such as cutting tax and fee, improving the business environment, and supporting the development of the real economy.

On the positive side, the economic structure continued to optimize in 2019. The share of the tertiary industry in the GDP increased to 53.9%, driving the growth of 13.52 million new jobs, exceeding the target of 11 million. Although the share of secondary industry in GDP decreased to 39.0%, the contribution rate of secondary industry to GDP growth increased to 36.8%, up 2.4 percentage points over the previous year. This reflected the structural adjustment and upgrading of industries, especially manufacturing industry, and the improvement of production efficiency. In addition, the consumption structure of residents was constantly optimized. The share of service consumption in residential consumption expenditure reached 50.2% in 2019, an increase of 0.7 percentage points over the previous year. The continuous optimization of consumption structure has promoted the transformation and upgrading of industrial structure and product structure from the demand side, and then improved the efficiency of growth. Finally, the investment in new energy grew rapidly, and the investment structure has gradually improved. The investment in high-tech industries grew rapidly, increasing by 17.3% in 2019, a rise of 2.4 percentage points over the previous year. The investment in high-tech manufacturing increased by 17.7%, an increase of 1.6 percentage points over the previous year, and it accounted for more than 20% of total manufacturing investment. In addition, investment in high-tech services increased by 16.5%, an increase of 3.6 percentage points over the previous year.

The growth rate of fixed asset investment, especially private investment continued to fall, which was the main reason for the economic downturn. The investment in fixed assets (excluding farmers) increased by 5.4% in 2019, down 0.5 percentage points over the previous year. The contribution rate of capital formation to GDP growth fell to 31.2%, a decrease of 10.3 percentage points over the previous year, the lowest in the past twenty years. The slow expansion of industrial production and the sharp decline of profit growth of industrial enterprises not only led to decline in the investment, but also inhibited the growth of tax revenue. In the whole year, industrial added value in real term of enterprises above designated size increased by 5.7%, down 0.5 percentage points over the previous year, and the total profits of enterprises above designated size contracted by 3.3%, a sharp decline of 13.6 percentage points over the previous year. In addition, the sharp rise in prices hindered the growth of real income and consumption of residents. "African swine fever" significantly increased the pork price, and the annual CPI rose to 2.9%, an increase of 0.8 percentage points over the previous year. On the other hand, the industrial producer price index (PPI) dropped from 3.5% in 2018 to 0.3% in 2019, owing to the decline of the international crude oil price and the slowdown in investment growth in the domestic market.

In order to cope with the downward pressure at home and from abroad, the Chinese government changed the ways of macro-control. In terms of monetary policies, while preventing financial risks and controlling leverage ratio, China has pushed forward the reform of the formation mechanism of the loan prime rate (LPR), which eliminated the lower limit of interest rate. While ensuring sufficient liquidity, China has increased the share of new RMB loans in the real economy.

In terms of the fiscal policies, China further implemented measures of tax reduction and fee reduction, in order to stabilize investment in manufacturing industry, and optimize the business environment. In addition, the financial investment in the new infrastructure and weak links improved the investment structure.

In 2020, the first phase economic and trade agreement between China and the US has laid a good foundation for both sides to ease and finally eliminate trade friction. At the same time, the continued implementation of loose monetary policies in major countries will lead to a rebound of global trade, and will drive the growth rate of private investment in manufacturing of China. However, the sudden outbreak of Covid-19 pandemic in the first quarter brought great impact to Chinese economy.

In the short term, the impact of the COVID-19 pandemic will pull down Chinese economic growth from supply side as well as demand side. The direct losses resulted from the decline of consumption expenditure during the Spring Festival, the demand suppression and production stagnation in most provinces especially Hubei Province. The secondary losses resulted from the decline of normal consumption demand due to pandemic prevention and control period, the different time of the resumption of work, production, and business activities, which damaged the normal supply chain and reduced production efficiency, and the damages of the normal supply of the global manufacturing industry chain due to the outbreak of the Covid-19 pandemic outside China.

Macroeconomic data released by the National Bureau of Statistics on March 16 show that the impact of the COVID-19 pandemic has led to a sharp decline in consumption of goods and services in January and February, a significant decline in the growth rate of industrial added value of enterprises above designated size and a sharp deceleration in fixed asset investment. In order to deal with the impact of the COVID-19 pandemic, Chinese government issued a series of hedging policies, which effectively boosted the resumption of work, production, and business activities.

However, there is still some uncertainty in the first and second quarter about the resumption of work, production and business activities, and the recovery of production capacity. Due to the slow growth of January and February of 2020, March will be an important month for the growth of the first quarter. After the outbreak of the COVID-19 pandemic outside China, economic growth in the second quarter will also face some downward pressure due to the cancellation of overseas orders. Based on this, our research team set the following three forecast scenarios, and applied the China's Quarterly Macroeconometric Model (CQMM) to forecast the main macroeconomic variables of China for the eight quarters in 2020 and 2021.

a. Optimistic scenario: small impact of external risk. It is assumed that from late February to March 2020, COVID-19 pandemic will be fully controlled. With full resumption of work and production and business activities, the average production capacity will be increased by 15% over last year. The second quarter can maintain normal productivity.

b. Benchmark scenario: medium impact of external risk. It is assumed that from late February to March 2020, COVID-19 pandemic prevention will be partially controlled. With a delay of the resumption of work and production and business activities, and production capacity can at most maintain the same level over last year; in the second quarter, industrial enterprises slowed production progress due to partial cancellation of oversea orders. At the same time, in order to offset the impact of the COVID-19 pandemic, domestic investment accelerated growth.

c. Pessimistic scenario: big impact of external risks. The impact of the COVID-19 pandemic outside China will restrain global demand and affect the normal supply of the global manufacturing industry chain in the first and even second quarter. Because most of the oversea orders of industrial enterprises have been cancelled, the production capacity cannot maintain the level of the same period of last year. At the same time, domestic investment will grow faster to offset the impact of the COVID-19 pandemic.

The forecasts based on CQMM models are as follows.[1]

1. **The growth rate of GDP**. In 2020, Chinese GDP growth rate will be 5.09, 4.59 and 3.18% under each of the three scenarios, down 1.06, 1.55 and 2.96 percentage points over the previous year, respectively. In the first quarter, GDP

[1]Unless otherwise specified, the growth rate of this paper is compared with that of the same period of last year.

growth rate will be 0.94%, −3.81% and −7.74%, respectively under the three scenarios; in the second quarter, it will rebound to 7.37–8.81%; in the third and fourth quarter, it will remain at 6.08–6.69% and 5.86–6.84%. In 2021, GDP growth will rebound to 6.6–8.24%.

2. **The growth rate of the fixed-asset investment**. In 2020, the growth rate of fixed-asset investment (excluding farmers) is expected be 6.60–8.49%, but will fall into the interval of −2.91–−7.26% in the first quarter. In term of ownership, in 2020, investment growth of state-owned and state-holding enterprises will be 7.28–11.26%, and the non-state-owned enterprises will remain in the range of 6.18–7.18%. In the first quarter, investment growth of state-owned and state-holding enterprises will fall to −1.44–−6.04%, and non-state-owned enterprises will fall to −3.91–−8.09%. It shows that the impact of the COVID-19 pandemic on the investment of non-state-owned enterprises is greater than that of state-owned and state-holding enterprises. Therefore, after the COVID-19 pandemic has been completely controlled, it is necessary to continue to implement the policies to ensure the financial to serve the real economy and to stabilize investment in manufacturing. In 2021, investment growth is expected to be 8.41–10.89%.
3. **CPI**. In 2020, CPI is expected to be 3.21–3.33%, exceeding the policy target of 3%, due to the impact of COVID-19 pandemic as well as the high pork price. CPI will be 5.09–5.24, 4.42–4.58, 2.84–2.99 and 0.52–0.71% in each of the four quarters. The rise of CPI will have negative impacts on the real income of the residents. In 2021, the base effect will put CPI down into the range of 0.27–0.38%.
4. **PPI**. PPI will decrease to −3.01–−3.54% in 2020, and hit the lowest point in the second quarter. With oil price fluctuations and the impact of the COVID-19 pandemic on industrial chain, PPI will continue to contract. In 2021, PPI will likely turn positive, increasing by 1.39–2.00%.
5. **The growth rate of retail sales**. In 2020, the nominal growth rate of total retail sales of social consumption goods is expected to be 4.48–7.58%. In the first quarter, it will drop into the interval of −0.14–−11.07%. In 2020, the growth rate of per capita disposable income will be in the intervals of 3.55–4.42, 4.51–6.44% for urban and rural residents, respectively. The impact of the COVID-19 pandemic and high pork prices, will erode the real income growth of the low-income residents. The policy should focus on stabilizing and increasing real income growth for the low-income residents. In 2021, gross retail sales of consumer goods will rise to 9.08–12.92%.
6. **The growth rate of imports and exports**. In 2020, the growth rate of total exports in China will remain at 2.28–4.45% in current dollar terms, and the growth rate of the total imports will be 6.33–11.76%. In term of countries or regions, the growth rate of exports to the US, the EU and ASEAN will be 8.79–9.41, 5.48–6.48, and 18.04–18.45%, respectively. The growth rate of imports from the US, the EU and ASEAN will be 10.64–11.73, 8.68–10.93 and 4.35–4.64%, respectively. In 2021, the growth rate of total exports will rise to 14.30–16.52%; the growth rate of total import growth will be 10.08–15.55%.

To sum up, Chinese economic growth rate will fall in 2020. The impact of the COVID-19 pandemic on investment of non-state-owned enterprises is greater than that of state-owned and state-holding enterprises; the impact on the real income of rural residents is greater than that of urban residents; and consumption will maintain a steady and positive trend. However, the impact of the COVID-19 pandemic is short-term and external. By strengthening hedging policies, and stimulating the vitality of enterprises, the losses caused can be minimized, and Chinese economy will develop steadily and healthily.

To achieve target of the "doubling GDP and doubling per capita income of residents over 2010" put forward by the Party's 18th National Congress, the growth rate of the GDP must be not less than 5.62% in 2020, but the predicted value is 5.08 instead of 5.62%. Therefore, if the policy focus of the first quarter is to boost the resumption of work, production, and business activities, to expand production capacity, and to ensure that the COVID-19 pandemic is fully controlled, then China should continue to strengthen hedging policies, and stimulate the vitality of enterprises, and promote the stable and healthy economic development.

So, what kind of momentum and macro policies are needed? Our research team proposes that, while continuing to implement prudent monetary policies, the market interest rate should be reduced by 20–60 basis points through the LPR reform; at the same time, with the increase growth rate of fiscal expenditure from 8.2% in 2019 to 15.3–15.8% in 2020, the GDP growth rate will increase to the targeted level of 5.62% even under the Benchmark scenario in 2020.

From the supply side, the LPR reform with a reduction of interest rate in the loan market can effectively stimulate the growth of private investment (price effect) which is more sensitive to the interest rate; and the reduction of interest rate will be conducive to strengthening the profit growth expectation and investment (cost effect) of private enterprises; The growth rate of private investment will be further increased under tax reduction policy. Consequently, the increase in the growth rate of private investment will be conducive to improving the investment structure and improving the efficiency of investment (effect of investment structure adjustment).

From the demand side, the reduction of interest rate of housing loan can strengthen the expectation (cost effect) of residential income; with expansion of fiscal expenditure, such as the tax reduction, increase of transfer income to residents and stability of the employment market, the growth of real income of residents will be stable, thus driving the growth of residential consumption.

Our research team made some assumptions on the LPR reform and the fiscal expenditure expansion, in order to analyze the comprehensive effects on Chinese economy of promotion of the LPR reform and expansion of the fiscal expenditure. The simulation results are as follows.

First, if the market interest rate can be reduced by 20–60 basis points and the growth rate of fiscal expenditure can be increased from 8.2% in 2019 to 15.3–15.8% in 2020, the targeted value of GDP growth of 5.62% can be achieved. In addition. If the growth rate of fiscal revenue will maintain at the same level of last year, 3.8%, the ratio of public fiscal deficit in GDP must be increased to 7.1% in 2020.

Second, under the same policy assumptions, the growth rate of private investment can be increased by 0.38 percentage points; the growth rate of urban fixed asset investment can be increased by 0.22 percentage points. As the growth rate of private investment is more sensitive to the interest rate, the effect of interest rate reduction will be more significant. Therefore, the policy combination of LPR reform and fiscal expenditure expansion will stabilize the growth of investment (total expansion effect), and improve the investment structure (structural adjustment effect).

Third, the interest rate of housing loans will not actually decline until 2021 (cost effect) due to the lag effect of the LPR reform. This will strengthen residential income growth expectation in 2021. At the same time, the expansion of fiscal expenditure can stabilize the growth of residential consumption through the reduction of tax in 2020, the increase of transfer income to residents and the expansion of employment security expenditure. In 2020, the nominal growth rate of total retail sales of consumption goods will increase by about 0.05–0.06 percentage points.

Based on the above analysis, our research team proposed that in 2020, in the face of the decline of economic growth, China should continue to adhere to the macro-control, such as the monetary and fiscal policies implemented in the previous years, adhere to various measures to prevent and control financial risks, to restrain the real estate, and strictly control the local government debt ratio; On the basis of the short-term policies to deal with the impact of the COVID-19 pandemic in the first quarter, China should further increase the momentum of policies to ensure that economic growth is stable while promoting economic restructuring.

First, China should continue to implement the prudent monetary policies. In 2020, while making every effort to do a good job in financial services for COVID-19 pandemic prevention, China should ensure that the share of loans to real economy is not less than 60%, and truly implement the requirements of financial services for the real economy. China should implement the reform of LPR, to improve the efficiency of market allocation of credit resources, to improve the investment structure and improve the investment efficiency. China should further give full play to the guidance role of credit policies to improve structure, ensure that funds are invested in advanced manufacturing, people's livelihood construction, infrastructure and other fields and promote the "double upgrading" of industry and consumption. At the same time, China should actively do a good job in financial support for employment and entrepreneurship, carry out financial targeted poverty alleviation and continue to strengthen financial support for industrial transformation and upgrading.

Second, China should appropriately speed up the growth of fiscal expenditure and focus on stabilizing the growth of the real income of residents. China should make full and flexible use of government bonds and various expenditure tools, appropriately accelerate the growth of public financial expenditure, appropriately expand the deficit, especially the central fiscal deficit, and improve the efficiency of the use of financial funds. The expansion of fiscal expenditure should be guided by strengthening people's livelihood, stabilizing the real income of residents, especially of low-income residents, and promoting the stable growth of consumption from the aspects of improving people's livelihood, social security, through measures such as tax reduction, increasing the transfer income to residents and ensuring the stability of the employment market. At the same time, China should further optimize the way of tax reduction and fee reduction by shifting from VAT reduction to income tax reduction. China should continue to push forward the investment in weak areas, such as the new type of infrastructure construction.

Third, the current policies of "stable investment" should focus on the long-term goal of "improving the competitiveness of enterprises". After the COVID-19 pandemic has been completely controlled, it is necessary to continue to implement the policies such as financial services for the real economy and stable manufacturing investment. However, the implementation of the policies should be able to squeeze out the inefficient investment, to promote the growth of effective investment, and to increase the demand of the domestic market; China should continue to deepen the reform of state-owned enterprises, implement competition neutrality and ownership neutrality, eliminate ownership discrimination, accelerate a fair competition business environment, improve the property rights protection system, expand the development space of the private economy, boost the confidence of enterprises, and stabilize the growth of private investment in the manufacturing industry. China should continue to increase the tax reduction for innovative enterprises and high-tech enterprises, and increase the R&D investment in order to achieve the sustained and rapid growth of labor productivity, China should encourage enterprises to expand R&D investment, enhance their innovation ability, increase the share of high-tech manufacturing industry, and accelerate the industrial transformation and product upgrading of manufacturing industry.

Fourth, China should pay more attention to the impact of the COVID-19 pandemic and the impact of food CPI on the real income of residents. Although the current economy does not have the basis of serious inflation, in the first half of 2020, the impact of the COVID-19 pandemic and the pork prices will keep CPI at a high level. Therefore, price stabilization is still a top priority. China should stabilize CPI growth by curbing the pork prices. At the same time, China should continue to implement the policy of tax reduction and fee reduction, increase the transfer income of low-income residents, accelerate the transfer of part of state-owned capital to enrich social security fund, ensure the stable decrease of social security rate, and ensure the growth of real income of residents, especially low-income residents.

Fifth, China should pay special attention to the relation between the industrial structure transformation and the employment promotion in order to achieve stable growth of employment, especially in high-income jobs. In recent years, with the increase of Chinese wage level, the proportion of labor-intensive manufacturing industry has declined rapidly, which aggravates the conflict between industrial structure transformation and employment promotion; At the same time, the high proportion of traditional service industry helps to promote employment, but most of the jobs are with low-income. Therefore, while stabilizing the total employment, China should improve the employment structure, improve the quality of employment, and ensure the stable growth of high-income jobs; while promoting the development of small and medium-sized enterprises (SMEs), China should give greater support to innovation, further strengthen vocational skills training, and accurately implement the employment work for key positions.

Contents

Chapter 1
China's Economic Performance in 2019

In 2019, the weakening of global trade expansion and the escalation of trade frictions between China and the US restrained the growth of private investment in Chinese manufacturing industry, the growth of profits of the industrial enterprises fell sharply, and the downward pressure on economic growth continued to increase. The growth rate of real gross domestic product (GDP) was 6.1%, down 0.6 percentage points over the previous year (see Fig. 1.1). In response to the downward pressure at home and from abroad, the Chinese government strengthened and improved macro-control policies and measures, such as reduction of tax and fee, improvement of business environment, and support for the real economy. Therefore, the national economy showed a trend of steady growth.

1.1 The Share of Secondary Industry to GDP Declined

In 2019, Chinese industrial production expansion slowed down. The share of the secondary industry in GDP continued to decline to 39.0%, the lowest in the past 20 years (see Fig. 1.2). At the same time, the share of the tertiary industry in GDP increased to 53.9%, and the share of primary industry was basically unchanged.[1]

In term the contribution rates in 2019, the contribution rate of the second industry to GDP growth increased to 36.8%, a rise of 2.4 percentage points over the previous year; the contribution rate of the tertiary industry to GDP growth decreased to 59.4%, down 2.1 percentage points over the previous year (see Fig. 1.3).

Since 2014, the contribution rate of the secondary industry to GDP growth has declined rapidly, and it has turned to recovery in recent two years. Whether this trend

[1]The continuous growth of the tertiary industry ensures the stable growth of employment. In 2019, 13.52 million new jobs will be created in cities and towns, exceeding the expected target of more than 11 million for seven consecutive years.

China's Macroeconomic Outlook, Current Chinese Economic Report Series,
https://doi.org/10.1007/978-981-15-9279-9_1

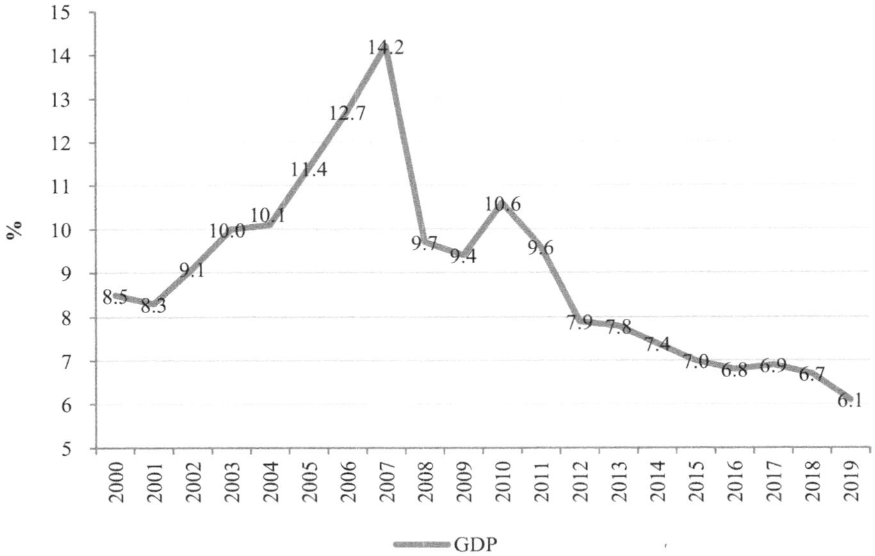

Fig. 1.1 The growth rate of real GDP. *Source* CQMM team calculations on CEIC data

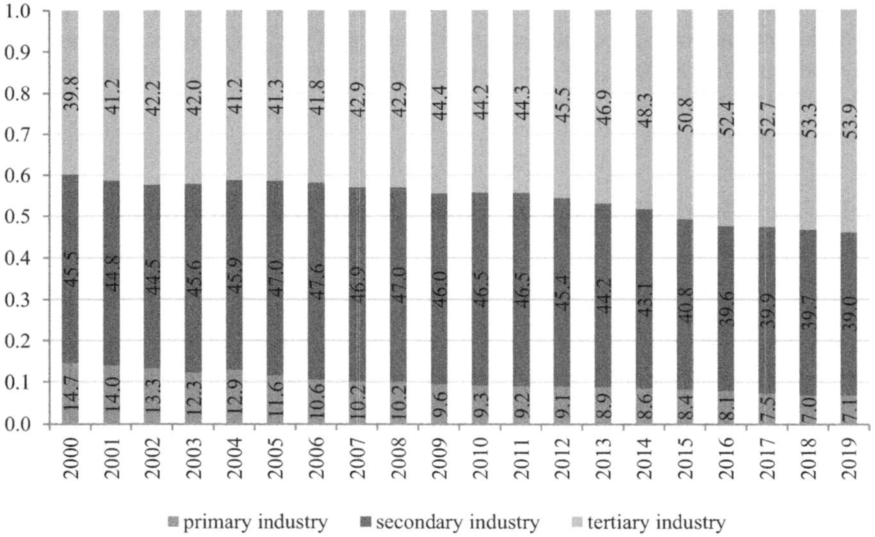

Fig. 1.2 The shares of the three industries in GDP. *Source* CQMM team calculations on CEIC data

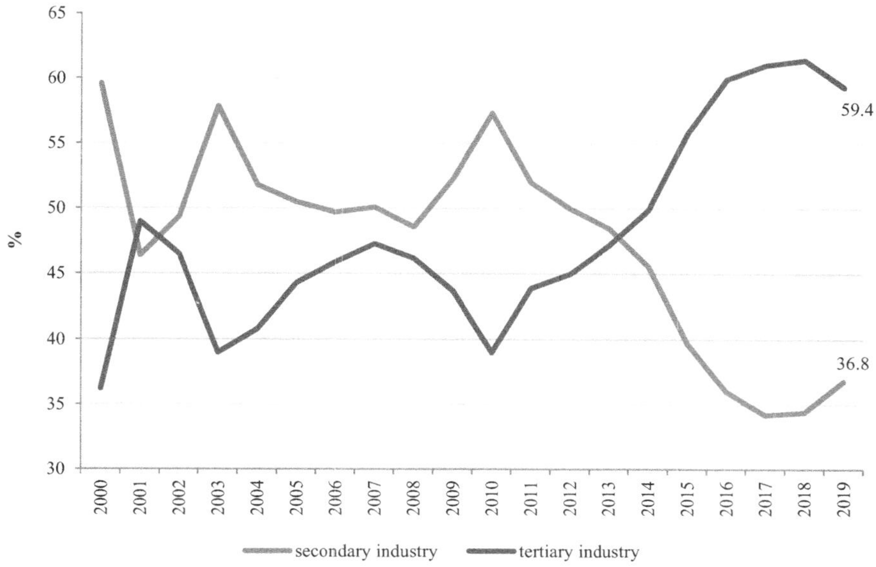

Fig. 1.3 The contribution rate to GDP growth. *Source* CQMM team calculations on CEIC data

can be sustained will depend on the adjustment of industrial structure, especially manufacturing industry, and the improvement of production efficiency.

In 2019, the growth rate of fixed asset investment continued to decline. The contribution rate of capital formation to GDP growth declined to 31.2%, down 10.3 percentage over the previous year, the lowest in the past 20 years. As the growth rate of real income of residents slowed down, the growth rate of consumption was difficult to increase rapidly. The contribution rate of final consumption to GDP growth declined to 57.8%, down 8.1 percentage points over the previous year. Despite the escalation of trade frictions between China and the US in 2019, the contribution rate of net exports of goods and services to GDP growth rose to 11.0%, up 18.4 percentage points over the previous year (see Fig. 1.4).

1.2 The Growth Rate of Fixed Asset Investment and Private Investment Declined

In 2019, the total social fixed asset investment (excluding farmers) increased by 5.4%, a decrease of 0.5 percentage points over the previous year (see Fig. 1.5). Since 2010, the investment growth rate has continued to decline. In term of ownership, the investment of state-owned and state-holding enterprises increased by 6.8%, up 4.9 percentage points over the previous year; the private investment increased by 4.7%, down 4.0 percentage points. The share of private investment in total investment was

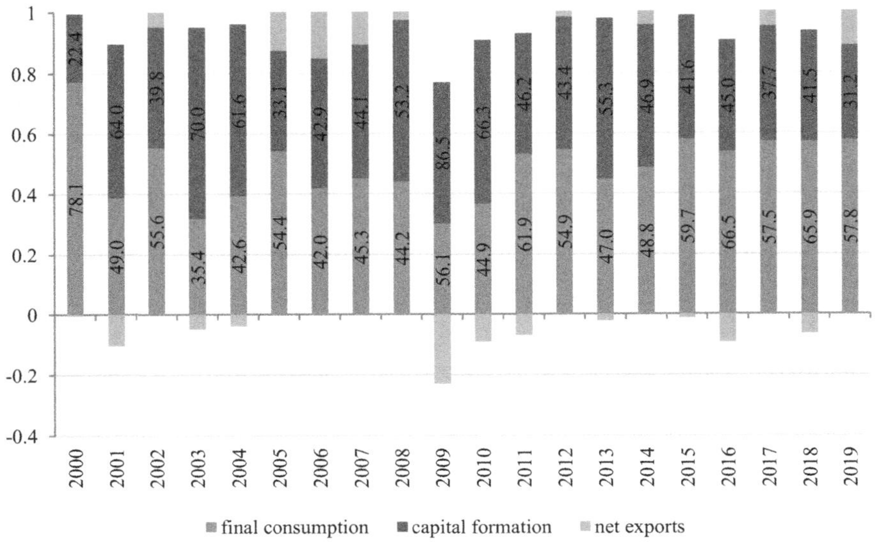

Fig. 1.4 The contribution rate to GDP growth, by expenditure method. *Source* CQMM team calculations on CEIC data

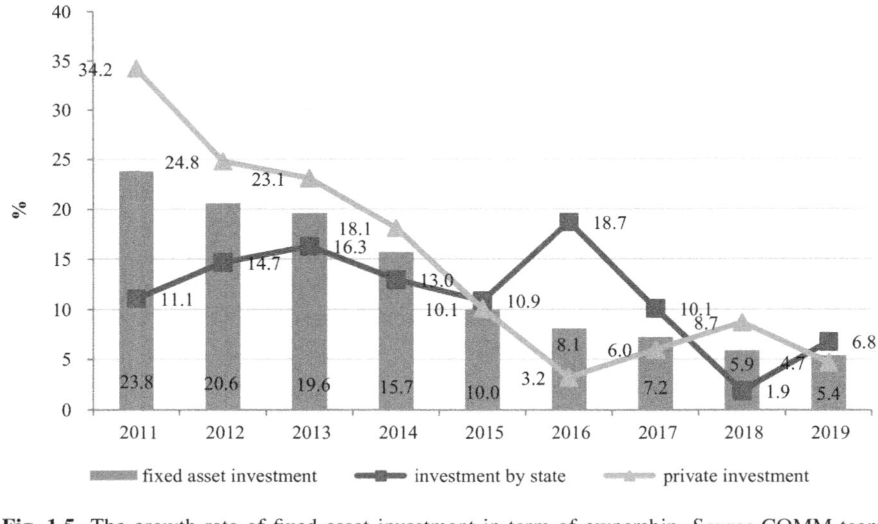

Fig. 1.5 The growth rate of fixed asset investment in term of ownership. *Source* CQMM team calculations on CEIC data

56.4%, down 5.6 percentage points, the lowest in the past decade. The growth rate of private investment, reached the bottom in 2016, increased in 2017 and 2018, but fell again in 2019 owing to trade friction between China and the US.

In 2019, the rebound in the manufacturing investment has stopped. The investment in manufacturing industry increased by 3.1%, a sharp decrease of 6.4 percentage points over the previous year, the lowest in the past 15 years (see Fig. 1.6). The strict implementation of policies to prevent financial risks and strengthen financial supervision has basically restrained the rapid growth of real estate investment and infrastructure investment. Real estate investment increased by 9.1%, a slight increase of 0.8 percentage points; infrastructure investment increased by 3.8%, which was the same as the previous year. The sharp decline of investment growth in manufacturing industry should be the main factor to restrain the growth of total investment.

Further, in term of the private investment in manufacturing industry (see Fig. 1.7), the investment grew at 2.8%, down 7.5 percentage points over last year. The cumulative growth rate in all months of 2019 fell sharply compared with the same period of last year. It shows that the slow expansion of global trade and the trade frictions between China and the US had a negative impact on Chinese export-oriented private manufacturing investment, and reversed its recovery trend since 2017.

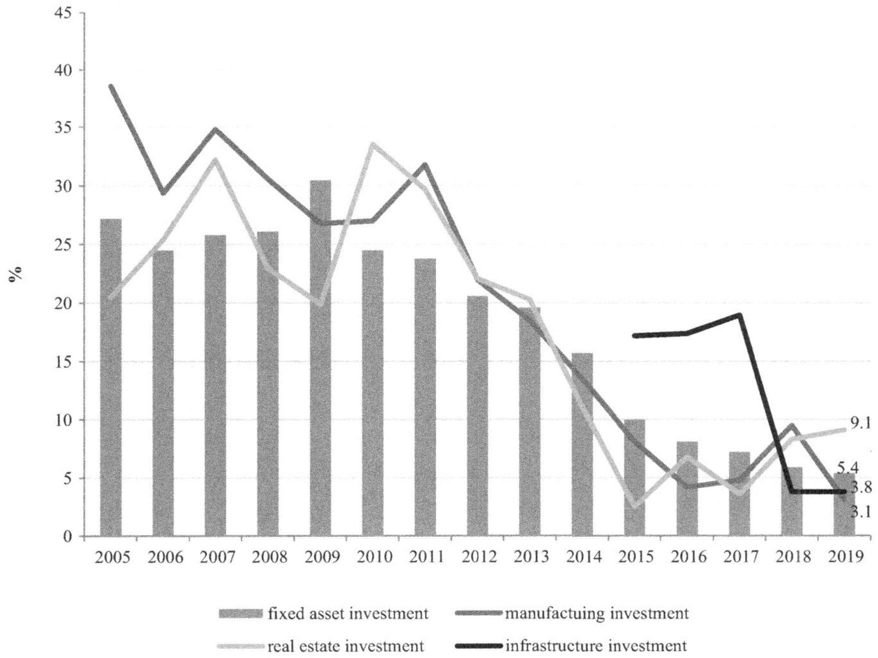

Fig. 1.6 The growth rates of investment of major industries. *Source* CQMM team calculations on CEIC data

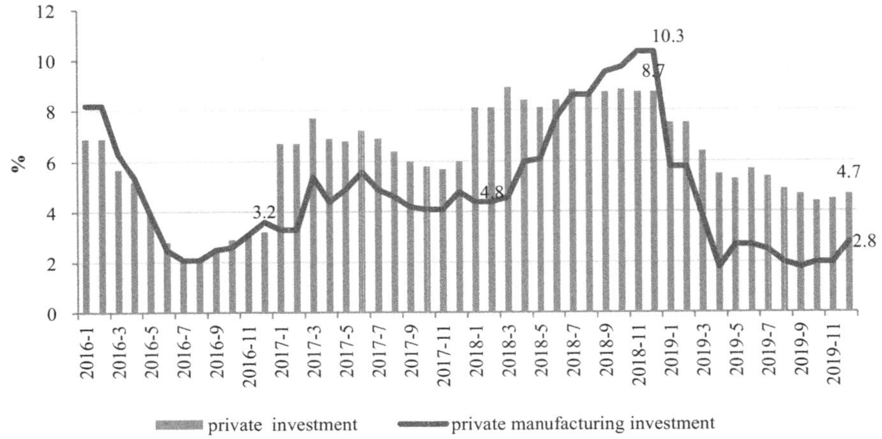

Fig. 1.7 The growth rate of commutative private investment. *Source* CQMM team calculations on CEIC data

In 2019, to response the continuous decline in investment growth, Chinese macro-control policies had changed greatly, such as tax reduction and fee reduction, improving the business environment, supporting the development of the real economy. The new energy investment grew rapidly, the investment in the weak areas continued to develop, and the investment structure was gradually improving. In 2019, investment in high-tech industry was growing rapidly, increasing by 17.3%, a rise of 2.4 percentage points over the previous year. Among them, investment in high-tech manufacturing increased by 17.7%, up 1.6 percentage points over the previous year, accounting for more than 20% of all manufacturing investment. In addition, investment in high-tech services increased by 16.5%, a rise of 3.6 percentage.

1.3 Production Grew Stably, the Growth Rate of Profit Declined Sharply

In 2019, the growth rate of industrial production is moderate and stable. The added value of industries above designated size in real term increased by 5.7%, a dropped of 0.5 percentage points over the previous year, the lowest in the past 20 years (see Fig. 1.8). Among them, the industrial added value of state-owned and state-holding enterprises increased by 4.8%, an decrease of 1.4 percentage points; the industrial added value of private enterprises increased by 7.7%, an increase of 1.5 percentage points; the industrial added value of foreign-funded and Hong Kong, Macao and Taiwan invested enterprises increased by 2.0%, an decrease of 2.8 percentage points. The growth rate of the industrial added value of private enterprises reached its lowest

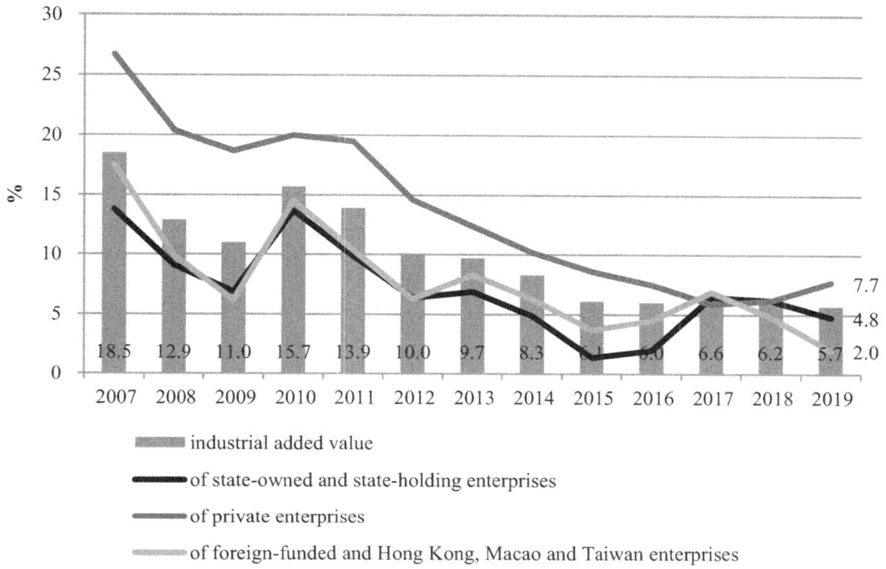

Fig. 1.8 The growth rate of real industrial added value of enterprises with ownership. *Source* CQMM team calculations on CEIC data

level of 5.9%, and the industrial added value of other types of ownership began to recover slightly for two consecutive years.

In term of industries, in 2019, the added value of the manufacturing industry increased by 6.0%, a decrease of 0.5 percentage points over the previous year (see Fig. 1.9). Among them, the added value of general equipment manufacturing, special equipment manufacturing, automobile manufacturing, computer, communication and other electronic equipment manufacturing increased by 4.3, 6.9, 1.8 and 9.3% respectively, down 2.9, 4.0, 3.1 and 3.8 percentage points over the previous year; The added value of the manufacturing of railway, ship, aerospace and other transportation equipment, electrical machinery and equipment manufacturing, and instrument manufacturing increased by 7.4, 10.7 and 10.5% respectively, up 2.1, 3.4 and 4.3 percentage points. In addition, the added value of high-tech manufacturing industry increased by 8.8%, a decline of 2.9 percentage points. The added value of high-tech manufacturing industry accounted for 14.4% of enterprises above designated size, only up 0.5 percentage points, which played a limited supporting role in the stable growth of industrial economy.

In 2019, the growth of profit of the industrial enterprises declined sharply. The total profits of industrial enterprises above designated size contracted by 3.3%, and the growth rate dropped by 13.6 percentage points compared with the previous year (see Fig. 1.10). In the past five years, the growth rate of profits of the industrial enterprises has rebounded rapidly from −2.3% in 2015 to 8.5% in 2016, to 21.0% in 2017, then decreased to 10.3% in 2018, and turned negative again in 2019. In

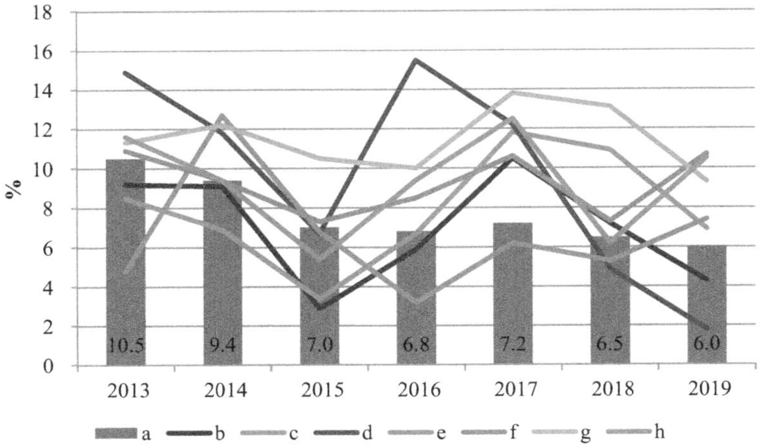

Fig. 1.9 The growth rate of industrial added value in real term. *Note a* The value added of manufacturing; *b* General equipment manufacturing; *c* Special equipment manufacturing industry; *d* Automobile manufacturing industry; *e* Railway, ship, aerospace and other transportation equipment; *f* Electrical machinery and equipment manufacturing; *g* Manufacturing of computer, communication and other electronic equipment; *h* Instrument manufacturing industry. *Source* CQMM team calculations on CEIC data

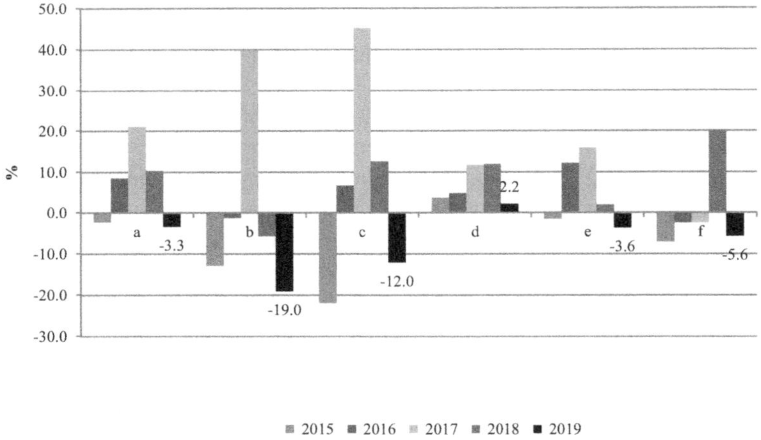

Fig. 1.10 The growth rate of total profits enterprises above designated size. *Note a* Industrial enterprises above designated size; *b* State-owned; *c* State-holding; *d* Private; *e* Foreign, Hongkong, Macao and Taiwan; *f* The rest. *Source* CQMM team calculations on CEIC data

terms of the ownership, the profit of state-owned enterprises decreased by 19.0%, a decrease of 13.3 percentage points over the previous year; the profit of state-holding enterprises decreased by 12.0%, an decrease of 24.6 percentage points; the profit of private enterprises increased by 2.2%, an increase of 9.7 percentage points; the profit of foreign and Hong Kong, Macao and Taiwan enterprises decreased by 3.6%, a decrease of 5.5 percentage points; Profits of other industrial enterprises decreased by 5.6%, a sharp decrease of 25.5 percentage points.

In 2019, the export was sluggish, and the export order index fell below the threshold value of 50. The impact of the global market had directly restrained the profit growth of the export-oriented manufacturing enterprises. The total profit of manufacturing enterprises grew by −5.2%, a drop of 13.9 percentage points compared with the previous year (see Fig. 1.11). Among them, the profits of general equipment manufacturing, special equipment manufacturing, automobile manufacturing and instrument manufacturing enterprises increased by 3.7, 12.9, −15.9 and 5.9% respectively; the profits of railway, ship, aerospace and other transportation equipment manufacturing, electrical machinery and equipment manufacturing, as well as computer, communication and other electronic devices increased by 11.9, 10.8 and 3.1% respectively.

In 2019, the weakening of global trade expansion and the escalation of trade frictions between China and the US have caused a great negative impact on Chinese

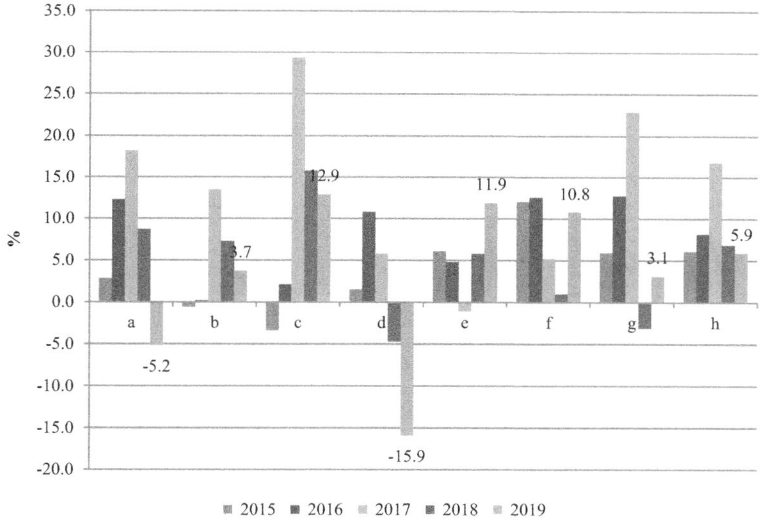

Fig. 1.11 The cumulative growth of total profits. *Note a* The added value of the manufacturing; *b* General equipment manufacturing; *c* Special equipment manufacturing industry; *d* Automobile manufacturing industry; *e* Railway, ship, aerospace and other transportation equipment; *f* Electrical machinery and equipment manufacturing; *g* Manufacturing of computer, communication and other electronic equipment; *h* Instrument manufacturing industry. *Source* CQMM team calculations on CEIC data

export-oriented manufacturing production. The rapid decline of the growth rate of the private investment in manufacturing industry and the general contraction of profit growth of all kinds of industrial enterprises had not only put downward pressure on economic growth, but also directly restrained the growth of fiscal revenue, thus weakening the ability of expansionary fiscal policies with tax reduction and fee reduction.

1.4 Imports and Exports Slowed Down, Share with the US Shrunk

In 2019, the growth rate of Chinese import and export of goods slowed down. The total export (RMB value) increased by 5.0%, a decrease of 2.1 percentage points over the previous year; the total import (RMB value) increased by 1.6%, a decreased of 11.3 percentage points. The trade surplus reached 2918 billion yuan, an increase of 593.29 billion yuan (see Fig. 1.12).

In term of countries or regions, in 2019, Chinese exports to the US accounted for 16.7% of the total exports, down 2.5 percentage points over the previous year; the exports to the European Union accounted for 17.1%, up 0.7 percentage points; the exports to ASEAN accounted for 14.4%, up 1.6 percentage points (see Fig. 1.13a).

Chinese imports from the US accounted for 5.9%, down 1.4 percentage points over the previous year; the imports from the European Union accounted for 13.4%, up 0.5 percentage points; the imports from ASEAN accounted for 13.6%, up 1.0 percentage points (see Fig. 1.13b).

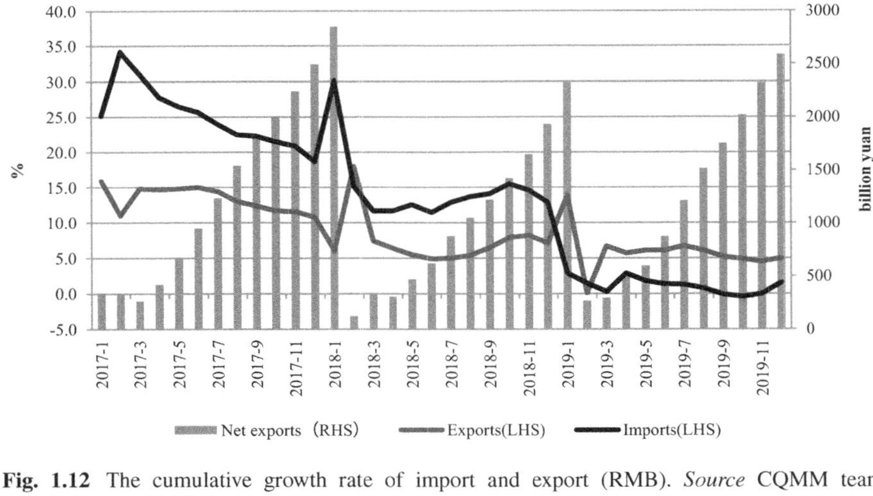

Fig. 1.12 The cumulative growth rate of import and export (RMB). *Source* CQMM team calculations on CEIC data

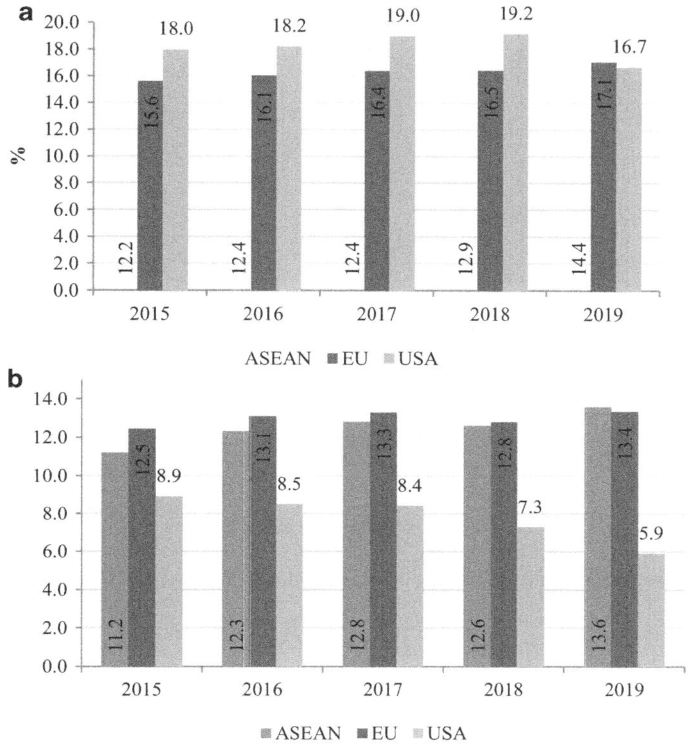

Fig. 1.13 **a** The export share to the major trading partners. **b** The import share from the major trading partners. *Source* CQMM team calculations on CEIC data

It shows that the escalation of trade frictions between China and the US had led to a significant decline in Chinese share of trade with the US, and the trade transfer effect had increased the share of trade between China and the European Union or ASEAN.

Affected by the escalation of trade frictions between China and the US, the exchange rate of US dollar against RMB once exceeded 7 in August 2019, and then fluctuated. By the end of 2019, the exchange rate was 6.976, about 1.9% lower than that of the beginning of the year (see Fig. 1.14). Since the central bank launched the reform of RMB exchange rate pricing mechanism in August 2015, the RMB exchange rate against the US dollar has maintained the trend of basic stability with fluctuation. At the end of the year, foreign exchange reserves totaled $3.11 trillion, nearly the same as the previous year.

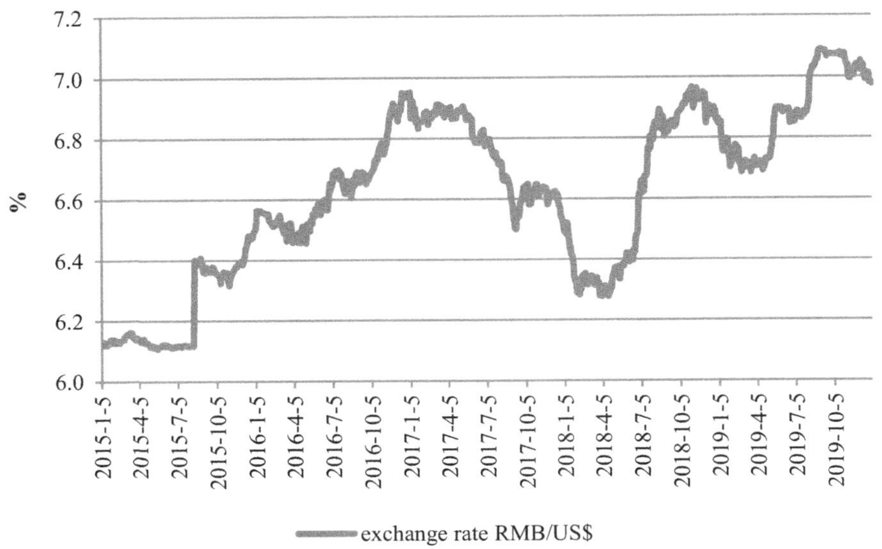

Fig. 1.14 The exchange rate of RMB against the US dollar. *Source* CQMM team calculations on CEIC data

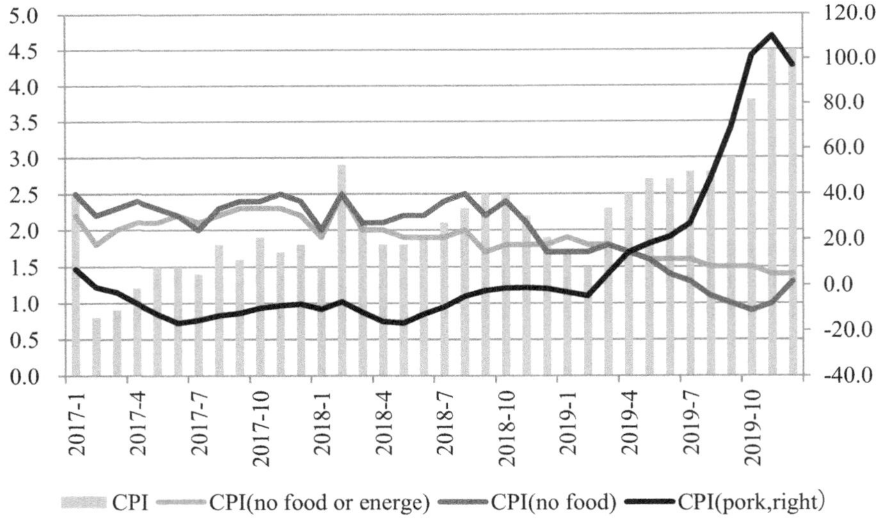

Fig. 1.15 The main indicators of CPI (last year = 100). *Source* CQMM team calculations on CEIC data

1.5 CPI Rose Sharply, PPI Dropped, the Growth of Consumption Slowed Down

In 2019, the impact of African swine fever greatly increased pork price. CPI rose 2.9% in 2019, up 0.8 percentage points over the previous year; core CPI excluding food and energy prices rose 1.6%, down 0.3 percentage points. On the other hand, the international crude oil price rose first and then fell, leading to the fall of the price of raw materials. Combined with the decline in the growth rate of investment in the domestic market, the producer price index (PPI) of the industry decreased by 0.3%, a decline of 3.8 percentage points (see Figs. 1.15 and 1.16).

In 2019, the growth of residential income continued to slow down slightly. The per capita real disposable income increased by 5.8%, down 0.7 percentage points, the lowest growth rate in the past five years. Among them, the per capita real disposable income of urban residents increased by 5.0%, a decreased of 0.6 percentage points. The per capita real disposable income of rural residents increased by 6.2%, a decreased of 0.4 percentage points (see Fig. 1.17).

In 2019, with the decline of growth rate of real income, the growth rate of consumption fell accordingly. The total retail sales of social consumption goods increased by 8.0% in nominal terms, down 1.0 percentage points. The total retail sales of social consumption goods increased by 6.0% in real terms, down 0.9 percentage points. The per capita consumption expenditure increased by 5.5% in real terms, down 0.7 percentage points; the per capita consumption expenditure of urban residents increased by 4.6% in real terms, the same as that of the previous year; the per capita

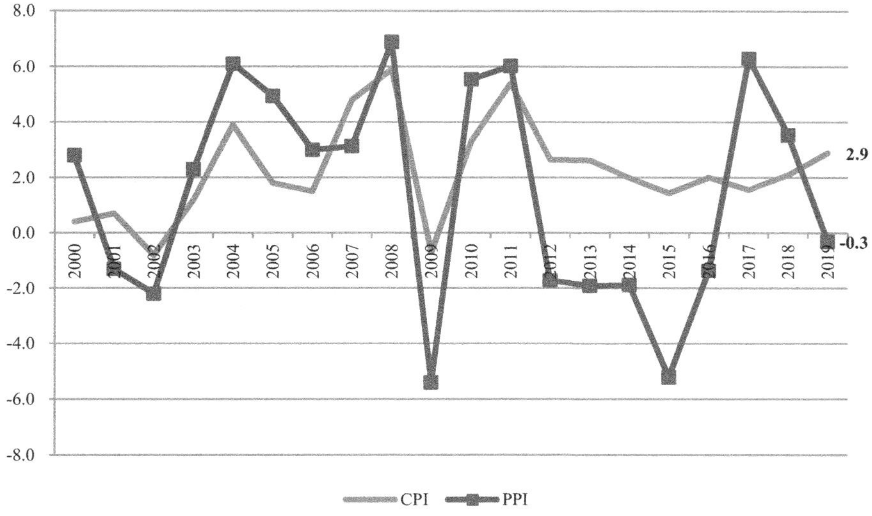

Fig. 1.16 The price indexes. *Source* CQMM team calculations on CEIC data

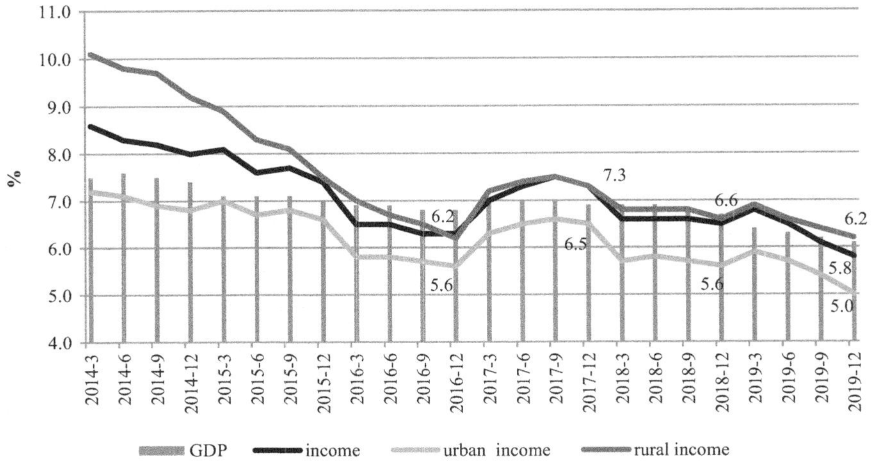

Fig. 1.17 The cumulative growth rates of GDP and per capita disposable income in real term. *Source* CQMM team calculations on CEIC data

consumption expenditure of rural residents increased by 6.5%, down 1.9 percentage points (see Fig. 1.18).

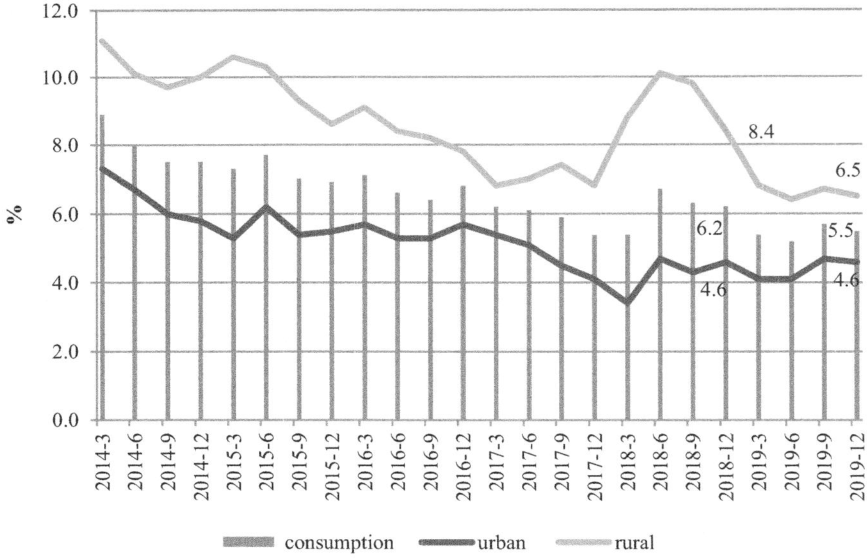

Fig. 1.18 The growth rate of cumulative consumption per capita in real term. *Source* CQMM team calculations on CEIC data

In recent years, the slow growth of Chinese labor productivity has restrained the rapid growth of real income of residents and the consumption. In the long run, with the accelerating the process of population aging, the growth rate of consumption expenditure was more difficult to increase rapidly. Therefore, the rapid growth of labor productivity in Chinese industry, especially in manufacturing industry should be the fundamental to ensure the labor productivity and then the rapid growth of the real income of residents.[2] How to expand the effective investment in manufacturing industry, promote industrial upgrading, and accelerate the growth of labor productivity is an important issue to be solved.

1.6 Monetary Policies Continued to Be Prudent

In 2019, while strictly preventing and controlling financial risks, the monetary policies remained prudent. Cash in circulation (M0) increased by 5.4% in the whole year, an increase of 1.8 percentage points over the previous year; M1 increased by 4.4%, an increase of 2.9 percentage points; M2 increased by 8.7%, an increase rate of 0.6 percentage points. The total amount of new social financing was 25.6 trillion yuan, an increase of 3.1 trillion yuan. Among them, RMB loans increased by 16.9 trillion yuan, an increase of 1.2 trillion yuan. The new RMB loans accounted for 66% of the total amount of new social financing, a decrease of 3.7 percentage points (see Fig. 1.19).

In 2019, among the new RMB loans, the real economy accounted for 56.2%, an increase of 4.8 percentage points over the previous year (see Fig. 1.20). Households accounted for 44.2%, down 1.3 percentage points; the proportion of loans to real estate also fell to 34.0%, down 5.9 percentage points.

Since 2016, the share of new RMB loans to real economy sharply decreased to 48.2%. This not only reduced the efficiency of the use of credit resources, but also inhibited the expansion of the investment demand of the real economy. At the same time, it aggravated the bubble of the real estate market and raised the systemic risk of the financial system. Since 2017, this share had recovered for three consecutive years. Although it still failed to reach the level of 63.0% of 2015, it shows that a series of policies on financial services for the real economy had improved the structure of new RMB loans.

In addition, based on the fundamental requirements of financial services for the real economy, monetary authorities should deepen the structural reform of the financial supply, and improve the transmission efficiency of the monetary policies.

The People's Bank of China (PBOC) started an interest rate reform on Aug 20, 2019, which we regard as a pragmatic start to unifying the "dual tracks" of interest rates—one for rates in the money market and the other for lending rates. Under the reform, the PBOC has improved the formation mechanism of the loan prime rate

---

[2]*China's macroeconomic forecast and analysis—spring report 2018*, by research team of the Research Center for Macroeconomic at Xiamen University.

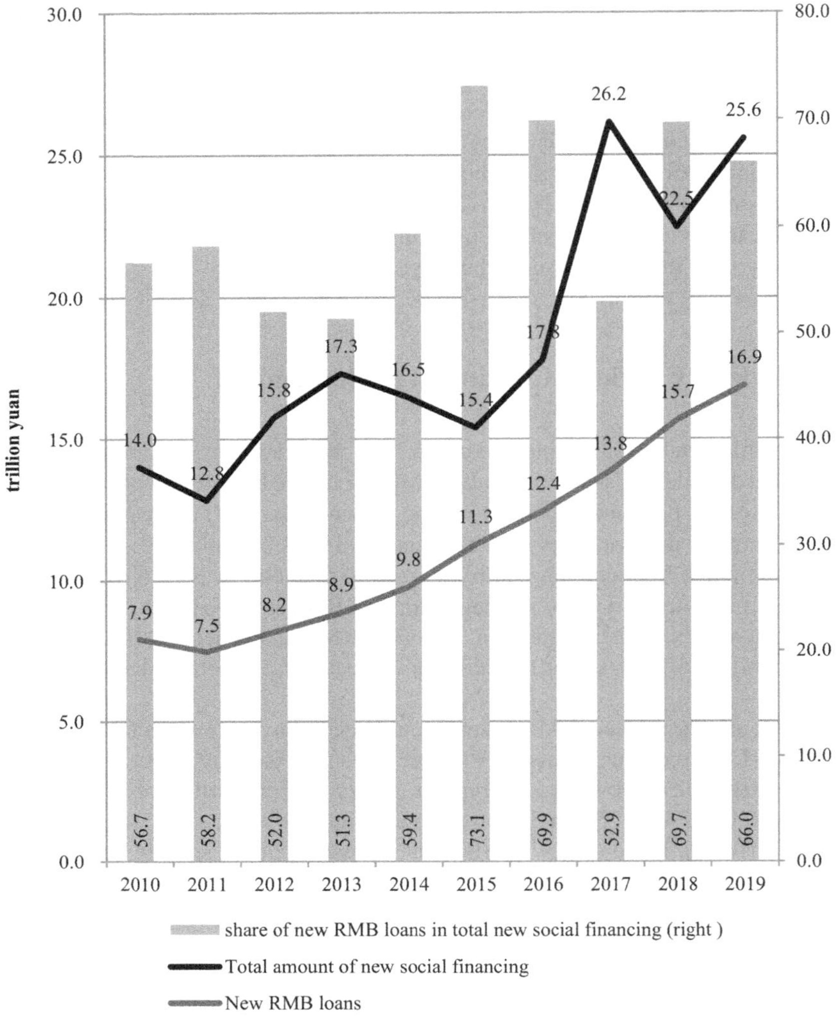

Fig. 1.19 The total amount of new social financing and new RMB loans. *Source* CQMM team calculations on CEIC data

(LPR), eliminating the lower limit of loan interest rate, and effectively reducing the interest burden of enterprises. At the same time, China increased financial support to small and micro enterprises, private enterprises of manufacturing industries. In 2019, the weighted interest rate of newly issued corporate loans was 5.12%, down about 0.48 percentage points over the previous year. At the end of the year, the LPR loan accounted for 90% of total loan.[3]

[3]People's Bank of China: monetary policy implementation report, No. 4, 2019.

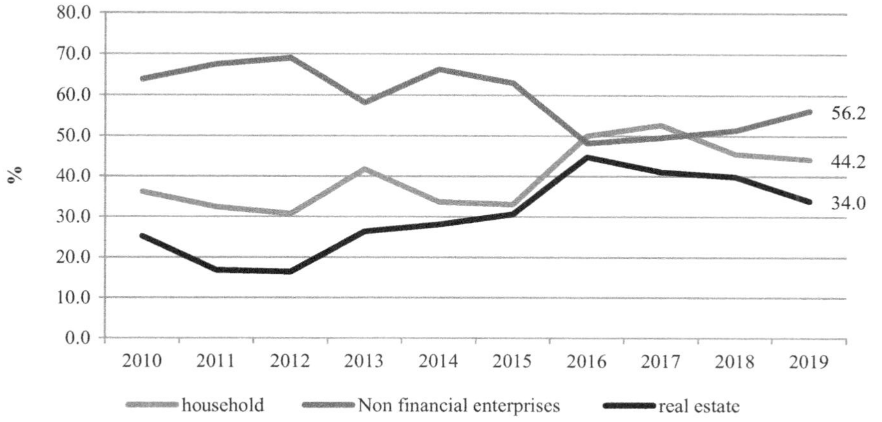

Fig. 1.20 The investment structure of new RMB loans. *Source* CQMM team calculations on CEIC data

1.7 Tax Revenue Slowed Down, and the Fiscal Expenditure Stable

In 2019, the nominal growth rate of general public budget revenue was 3.8%, down 2.4 percentage points over the previous year; the nominal growth rate of general public budget expenditure was 8.1%, down 0.6 percentage points (see Fig. 1.21). Affected by the sharp decline of profit growth of industrial enterprises above designated size, the growth rate of tax revenue declined significantly. The annual tax revenue increased by 1.0%, a decrease of 7.3 percentage points; the tax revenue accounted for 83.0% of the general public budget revenue, down 2.3 percentage points. The revenue from the state-owned land of local governments was about 7.3 trillion yuan, growing by 11.4%, a decrease of 13.6 percentage points.

In 2013, the growth rate of tax revenue declined from the double-digit to single digit, and it dropped to 4.3% in 2016, it rebounded to 10.7% in 2017 and dropped to 1.0% in 2019, the lowest in the past 30 years. Under the financial and tax system with VAT as the main source of tax, the slowdown of industrial production, the contraction of PPI and the decline of the growth rate of corporate profits had greatly inhibited the growth of tax revenue. In order to ensure the fiscal revenue, local governments had to increase the price of land, obtain loan resources through land mortgage by restricting land supply. This directly increased the debt burden of local governments, and then expanded the risk of the financial system.

Although the growth rate of fiscal revenue continued to decline, fiscal expenditure rose stably. By introducing a series of policies and measures, such as reducing taxes and fees, improving the business environment, supporting the development of the real economy, especially stabilizing the investment in the manufacturing industry, the investment structure had been improved while the economic growth had been stabilized, and the economic transformation and upgrading trend had been continued.

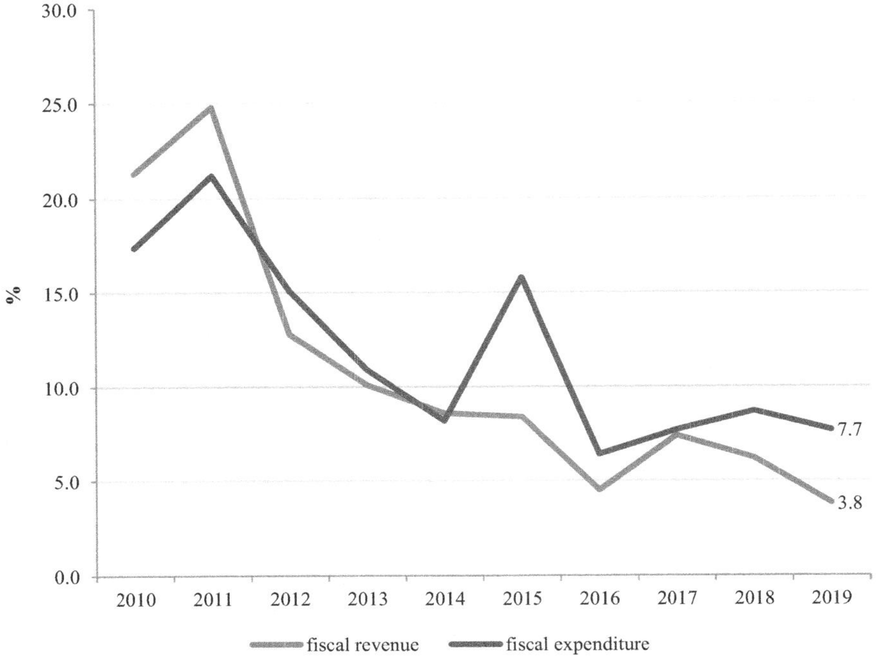

Fig. 1.21 The growth rate of general public budget revenue and expenditure. *Source* CQMM team calculations on CEIC data

First of all, greater tax reduction and fee reduction policies had reduced the burden of enterprises. In 2019, more than 2 trillion yuan of tax reduction and fee reduction had been added. Among them, the social security expenses of enterprises were reduced by 425.2 billion yuan. Greater efforts had been made to reduce taxes and fees, and optimize the business environment by reducing the burden of enterprises, enhancing the vitality of micro enterprises, and improving the operation of private and small and micro enterprises. Secondly, reduction of tax and expansion of transfer income of residents had stabilized the growth of residential income. The special deduction policy of personal income tax issued at the beginning of 2019 has deducted six major items and reduced the tax burden of residents. The per capita net transfer income of residents increased by 9.9%, up 1.0 percentage points over the previous year; the proportion of net transfer income in disposable income was 18.5%, up 0.2 percentage points. Among them, the per capita net transfer income of urban residents increased by 8.2%, up 1.1 percentage points; the proportion of the net transfer income in the per capita disposable income of urban residents was 17.9%, up 0.1 percentage points. The per capita net transfer income of rural residents increased by 12.9%, up 0.7 percentage points; the proportion of the net transfer income in the per capita disposable income of rural residents was 20.6%, up 0.6 percentage points. Finally, China will continue to work hard to improve the investment structure, to protect the environment. In some weak links, such as ecological protection and environmental governance, investment achieved rapid growth.

To sum up, global trade continued to decline in 2019. The growth rate of global trade in goods and services was 1.0%, a decrease of 2.6 percentage points over the previous year. Among them, the trade of developed countries increased by 1.3%, a decrease of 1.9 percentage points. The trade of emerging and developing countries increased by 0.4%, a decrease of 4.2 percentage points.[4]

Affected by this, the growth rate of Chinese industrial export delivery value continued to grow negatively from August to November 2019. In December, the growth rate returned to 0.4%. The slowdown of global trade expansion and the escalation of trade frictions between China and the US restrained the growth of private investment in export-oriented manufacturing industry, and the profit growth of industrial enterprises shrunk. In order to cope with the increasing downward pressure on the economy, while continuing to implement the prudent monetary policies, the financial policies increased efforts to promote tax reduction and fee reduction, ensuring the overall smooth operation of the national economy, improving the quality of development, and laying a solid foundation for building a moderately prosperous society in all respects by 2020.

In 2020, China and the US reached the first phase of trade agreement in mid-January, which strengthened the expectation that China and the US will avoid further escalation of trade frictions. In January 2020, the International Monetary Fund (IMF) predicted that the global economic growth will increase from 2.9% in 2019 to 3.3% in 2020 and 3.4% in 2021.

There are three main favorable factors supporting the growth of global economy: first, the monetary policies of major countries continue to be loose; China US trade negotiations are getting better; the rebound in manufacturing activities and global trade is also an important factor. The IMF forecasts that the growth rate of global trade in goods and services will rebound to 2.9 and 3.7% in 2020 and 2021 respectively. Among them, in 2020, the trade of developed countries, emerging and developing countries will grow by 2.2 and 4.2%, respectively. The rebound of global trade will greatly strengthen the investment of Chinese export-oriented manufacturing industry and improve the profit growth prospects of manufacturing enterprises.

The outbreak of the COVID-19 pandemic in late January, however, has great impact on the Chinese economic growth in 2020. In response to the COVID-19 pandemic, prevention and control measures have been taken, such as isolation of residents at home and delay of resumption of work, production, and business activities. By the end of February, although the COVID-19 pandemic has begun to decline, in order to prevent the recurrence of the COVID-19 pandemic, all provinces maintain different control efforts and take different time to resume the work, production, and business activities according to the actual situation. The negative impact of the COVID-19 pandemic on Chinese economy in the first quarter of 2020 and the first half of the year cannot be ignored.

[4] International Monetary Fund (IMF): world economic outlook, January 2020.

2020 is the year of the building a moderately prosperous society of China in all respects and the last year of the 13th five-year-plan. Though the Chinese economic will grow stably in the long run, the downward pressure on the economy is still large in the short run.

In 2019, the Chinese government's macro-control mode has fundamentally changed in response to the declining growth rate of private investment due to the impact of the global market. In terms of the monetary policies, based on the fundamental requirements of financial services for the real economy, the monetary policies adheres to the "stable" tone, at the same time, by deepening the structural reform of the financial supply, reforming the formation mechanism of the loan prime rate (LPR), reducing the interest burden of the real economy, and improving the price transmission efficiency of the monetary policies; while maintaining reasonable and abundant liquidity, China should improve the investment structure of credit resources, steadily increase the share of new RMB loans to the real economy; increase financial support to private, small and micro enterprises.

In 2019, in terms of the fiscal policies, the burden of enterprises had been effectively reduced and the vitality of micro enterprises had been strengthened through greater tax reduction and fee reduction and the optimization of business environment; the special additional deduction policy of personal income tax and the strengthening of the growth of net transfer income to the residents had stabilized the growth of disposable income of residents; more importantly, and some policies and measures to stabilize the investment in manufacturing industry ensure the rapid growth of new energy investment and the investment structure is gradually optimized. These measures will be able to continuously consolidate the foundation of Chinese economic growth and promote the orderly transformation of growth momentum.

China must adhere to the new development concept and promote the development of high quality. China must adhere to the structural reform of supply side, persist in reform and opening up. China must ensure stability on the six fronts and security in the six areas, and ensure stable economic performance is of crucial significance. China need to pursue reform and opening up as a means to stabilize employment, ensure people's wellbeing, stimulate consumption, energize the market, and achieve stable growth. China need to blaze a new path that enables us to respond effectively to shocks and sustain a positive growth cycle.

In 2020, it is an important part of deepening the reform of interest rate and improving the formation mechanism of the loan prime rate (LPR) in the loan market. This can not only reduce the loan interest rate of enterprises, but also help to improve the efficiency of market allocation of credit resources. At the same time, in terms of the fiscal policies, while the supply side continues to implement policies such as tax reduction and fee reduction and optimization of business environment, it is also necessary to increase the incentive of the demand side to the residential sector, and stabilize the income growth of residents, especially rural residents, through tax reduction, expansion of transfer income and stabilization of the employment market. Therefore, it is necessary to make full use of government bonds and all kinds of expenditure tools, appropriately increase the ratio of fiscal deficit to GDP, activate the financial stock funds, and improve the efficiency of the use of financial funds.

Through the above monetary and fiscal policies, it is expected that in 2020, while stabilizing growth and achieving the goal of doubling, China will vigorously promote economic restructuring and improve growth efficiency. Based on this, this report attempts to analyze the possible macroeconomic effects of LPR reform and fiscal expenditure expansion using China's Quarterly Macroeconometric Model (CQMM model).

Chapter 2
Quarterly Forecast for 2020–2021

2.1 Assumptions on the Exogenous Variable

2.1.1 Economic Growth Rates of the US and the Euro Area

In 2019, the prevalence of US trade protectionism has not only severely inhibited the growth of global trade, but also slowed down the growth of US private consumer spending. As the effect of the large-scale fiscal stimulus in the early stage has weakened, although the Federal Reserve cut interest rates three times in the year, the US economy grew by 2.3%, the lowest in nearly three years, less than the target of 3% set by the Trump administration. In the short term, the US economic growth is expected to continue to decline, due to the weakening effect of large-scale fiscal stimulus in the early stage, the narrowing space of the monetary policies, and the rising of geopolitical tensions. According to the World Economic Outlook updated by the International Monetary Fund (IMF) in January 2020, the US economy will grow by 2.0% in 2020, a decrease of 0.3 percentage points over the previous year, and it will further decline to 1.7% in 2021.[1]

On the other hand, the rebound of global trade growth will boost the growth of Germany's manufacturing industry. The final conclusion of the BREXIT will largely eliminate the uncertainty of economic growth in the Euro area. With the continuation of the effect of early loose monetary policies, it is expected that the Euro area will maintain a slow recovery in the next two years. In January, the IMF predicted that the economy of the Euro area will grow by 1.3% in 2020, a slight increase of 0.1 percentage point over the previous year, and may further rise to 1.4% in 2021.

[1]On February 22, 2020, the IMF forecast value of China's economic growth rate to be 5.6% in 2020, which was 0.4 percentage points lower than the forecast value of the world economic outlook updated in January; meanwhile, it lowered the forecast value of global economic grow rate to be 3.2% in 2020, which was 0.1 percentage points lower than the forecast value of the world economic outlook updated in January.

China's Macroeconomic Outlook, Current Chinese Economic Report Series,
https://doi.org/10.1007/978-981-15-9279-9_2

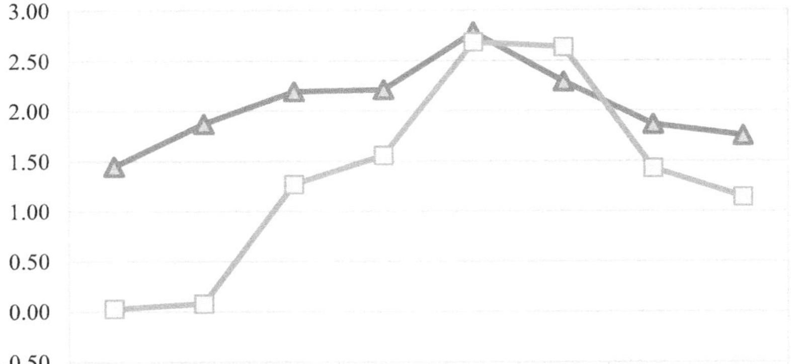

	2020Q1	2020Q2	2020Q3	2020Q4	2021Q1	2021Q2	2021Q3	2021Q4
USGDP_C	1.45	1.87	2.19	2.21	2.78	2.29	1.86	1.75
EAGDP_C	0.03	0.08	1.27	1.56	2.69	2.64	1.43	1.14

Fig. 2.1 Assumptions on the growth rate of the US and the Euro. *Note* USGDP_C refers to GDP growth rate of the United States, EAGDP_C represents GDP growth in the Euro area. *Source* CQMM team assumptions

Considering the positive impact of the first phase of China US economic and trade agreement in 2020, the short-term negative impact of the COVID-19 pandemic, and the possible hedging policies adopted by major countries, our research team adjusted the forecast values of the International Monetary Fund (IMF) for the US and Euro area economy on January 20, 2020, **assuming that in the next two years, the growth rate of the US is 1.93 and 2.17%, and the growth rate of the Euro area is 1.18 and 1.52%, and the corresponding quarterly growth rate is set as Fig.** 2.1.

2.1.2 The Exchange Rates

Based on the above forecast of the slowdown of the US economic growth, it is expected that the US dollar will continue to weaken in the next two years. It is assumed that the exchange rate of Euro against US dollar will gradually increase from 1.11 in the first quarter of 2020 to 1.16 in the fourth quarter of 2021 (see Fig. 2.2). On the other hand, affected by the impact of the COVID-19 pandemic, the exchange rate of RMB against US dollar in the first quarter of 2020 will be close to 7.01; as the decline of COVID-19 pandemic, the RMB will begin to gradually appreciate, reaching 6.72 by the end of 2021 (see Fig. 2.2).

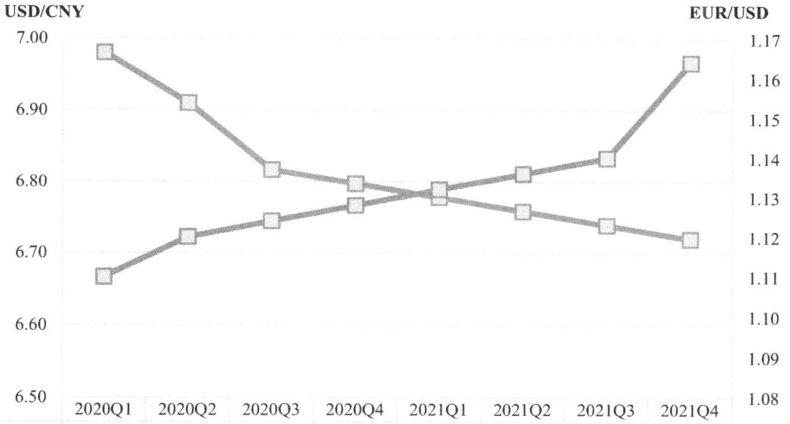

	2020Q1	2020Q2	2020Q3	2020Q4	2021Q1	2021Q2	2021Q3	2021Q4
USD/CNY	6.98	6.91	6.82	6.80	6.78	6.76	6.74	6.72
EUR/USD	1.11	1.12	1.12	1.13	1.13	1.14	1.14	1.16

Fig. 2.2 Assumptions on changes in exchange rates. *Note* USD/CNY is the exchange rate between us dollar and RMB, and EUR/USD is the exchange rate between Euro and US dollar. *Source* CQMM team assumptions

2.1.3 Growth Rate of the Broad Money Supply (M2)

At the end of 2019, the growth rate of M2 and social financing increased by 8.7 and 10.7% respectively, both of which were slightly higher than the nominal growth rate of GDP. The outbreak of COVID-19 pandemic temporarily caused negative impact on Chinese economy recently, but the long-term trend of economic growth will not change. Based on this, it is expected that the monetary policies will continue to maintain a stable and flexible tone in the next two years. Our research team assumes that the growth rate of M2 will be 8.85 and 8.35% in 2020 and 2021 respectively (see Fig. 2.3). At the same time, with the LPR reform, the interest rate, especially the loan interest rate of small and micro enterprises, is expected to gradually decline.

2.2 Scenario Design of Model for Prediction

In 2020, the signing of the first phase of the economic and trade agreement between China and the US laid a good foundation for the two sides to ease and eventually eliminate trade frictions. At the same time, the implementation of loose monetary policies in major countries is expected to lead to a rebound of global trade. The outbreak of COVID-19 pandemic in China in 2020 has brought a great impact to Chinese economy in the first quarter. The outbreak of COVID-19 pandemic outside

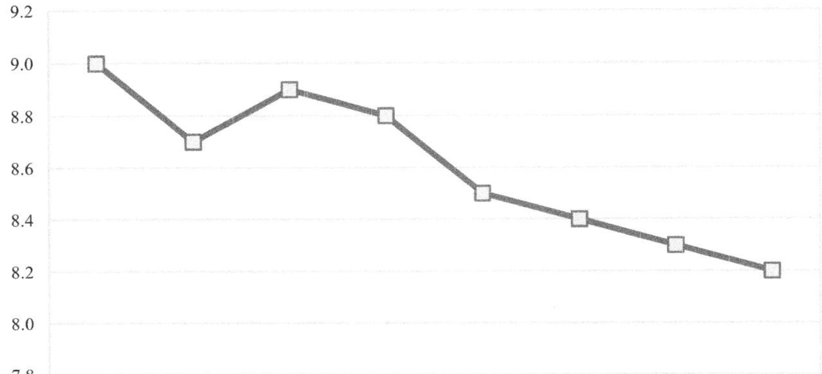

	2020Q1	2020Q2	2020Q3	2020Q4	2021Q1	2021Q2	2021Q3	2021Q4
M2	9.00	8.70	8.90	8.80	8.50	8.40	8.30	8.20

Fig. 2.3 Assumptions on M2 growth rates. *Source* CQMM team assumptions

China will further form downward pressure on Chinese economic growth through trade channels.

In the short term, the impact of the COVID-19 pandemic will slowdown Chinese economic growth from both supply side and demand side. The direct losses resulted from the decline of consumption expenditure during the Spring Festival, the demand suppression and production stagnation in most provinces especially Hubei Province. The secondary losses resulted from the decline of normal consumption demand due to pandemic prevention and control period, the different time of the resumption of work, production, and business activities, which damaged the normal supply chain and reduced production efficiency, and the damages of the normal supply of the global manufacturing industry chain due to the outbreak of the Covid-19 pandemic outside China.

The macro-economic data of January February 2020 released by the National Bureau of Statistics shows that the impact of the COVID-19 pandemic has led to a sharp decline in the consumption of goods and services in January and February, a significant decline in the growth rate of added value of industries above designated size, and a significant slowdown in fixed asset investment.[2] In response to the impact of the COVID-19 pandemic, the Chinese government issued a series of hedging policies, which effectively boosted the resumption of work, production, and business activities, while maximizing support for COVID-19 pandemic prevention and control.

However, there are still some uncertainties in the first quarter and the second quarter about the progress of the resumption of work, production, and business activities and the capacity recovery. Based on the economic data released by the National Bureau of Statistics, the GDP of January and February accounts for only 60% of GDP of the first quarter, which meant that March will be very important for the growth of

[2]https://www.stats.gov.cn/tjsj/zxfb/202003/t20200316_1732232.html.

the first quarter. After the outbreak of the COVID-19 pandemic outside China, the economic growth in the second quarter will also face some downward pressure due to the cancellation of overseas orders. Based on this, three prediction scenarios are set as follows:

a. **Optimistic scenario: small impact of external risk.** It is assumed that from late February to March 2020, COVID-19 pandemic prevention basically was fully controlled. With full resumption of work and production and business activities, the average production capacity will be increased by 15% over last year. The second quarter can maintain normal production progress.
b. **Benchmark scenario: medium impact of external risk.** It is assumed that from late February to March 2020, COVID-19 pandemic prevention basically was partially controlled. With a delay of the resumption of work and production and business activities, and capacity can at most maintain the same level over last year; in the second quarter, industrial enterprises slowed production progress due to partial cancellation of oversea orders. At the same time, in order to offset the impact of the COVID-19 pandemic, domestic investment accelerated growth.
c. **Pessimistic scenario: big impact of external risks.** The impact of the COVID-19 pandemic outside China is beginning to restrain global demand and affect the normal supply of the global manufacturing industry chain in the first and even second quarter. Because most of the oversea orders of industrial enterprises have been cancelled, the production capacity cannot maintain the level of the same period of last year. At the same time, domestic investment will grow faster to offset the COVID-19 pandemic.

Our research team applied the China's Quarterly Macroeconometric Model (CQMM) to predict the main economic indicators of China for the eight quarters in 2020 and 2021.

2.3 Forecasts of Main Economic Indicators in 2020–2021

2.3.1 The Growth Rate of GDP

With the exogenous assumptions, the forecast based on the CQMM are as follows.

Under the optimistic scenario, Chinese GDP growth will decline to 5.09% in 2020, down 1.06 percentage points; in 2021, with the base effect, the GDP growth will rebound to 6.61%. From the perspective of quarterly growth, under the optimistic scenario, in the first quarter of 2020, GDP growth rate will decline to 0.94%; with the COVID-19 pandemic under full control in the second quarter and with the rebound in demand and supply, the growth rate of GDP in the second quarter will reach 7.37%. The growth rate in the third and fourth quarters of 2020 will be 6.08 and 5.86%. The growth rate of GDP in each quarter of 2021 will be high in the beginning and low in the end (see Fig. 2.4).

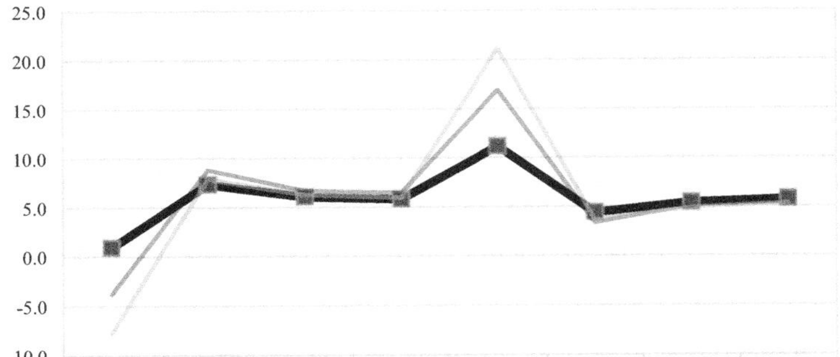

	2020q1	2020q2	2020q3	2020q4	2021q1	2021q2	2021q3	2021q4
GDP_C_SA	0.94	7.37	6.08	5.86	11.17	4.42	5.42	5.77
Risk scenario 1	-3.81	8.81	6.69	6.48	16.92	3.35	5.09	5.42
Risk scenario 2	-7.74	7.90	6.31	5.99	21.17	3.64	4.87	5.34

Fig. 2.4 Projectedquarterly growth rate of GDP. *Note* Risk scenario 1 and Risk scenario 2 refer to Benchmark scenario and pessimistic scenario. *Source* CQMM team calculations

Under the Benchmark scenario, if the resumption of work, production, and business activities is postponed, the impact of COVID-19 pandemic outside China is large, and overseas orders and production capacity can only maintain the average level of the same period of last year, then in the first quarter of 2020, the growth rate of GDP will fall sharply to −3.81%. In 2020, the annual growth rate of GDP will decline to 4.59%, down 1.55 percentage points over the previous year.

Under the pessimistic scenario, the significant impact of the outbreak of COVID-19 pandemic outside China, in the first quarter of 2020, the growth rate of GDP may drop to −7.74%. In 2020, the annual growth rate of GDP will further fall to 3.18%, down 2.96 percentage points over the previous year.

The outbreak of the COVID-19 pandemic has a strong impact on the Chinese economy in the first quarter of 2020. The annual GDP growth will slow down significantly. Although the impact of the COVID-19 pandemic on Chinese economy is temporary, in order to achieve the goal of stable growth and high-quality economic development, the implementation of Chinese macro policies in the next two years will face greater challenges.

2.3.2 *The Growth Rate of Investment*

In 2019, influenced by the slowdown of global trade, the growth rate of Chinese fixed asset investment continued to decline, especially in the private manufacturing industry. In 2020, the rebound of global trade growth and the smooth progress of China and the US trade negotiations are expected to stabilize and enhance the investment growth of private manufacturing industry. The impact of the COVID-19

Table 2.1 Forecast of investment growth rate (current price) from 2020 to 2021: %

Variables	Scenario	2020				2021				2020	2021
		Q1	Q2	Q3	Q4	Q1	Q2	Q3	Q4		
Invest 1	Optimistic	−4.09	9.45	6.13	2.22	11.78	0.76	3.07	4.44	3.40	4.82
	Benchmark	−6.72	14.45	8.16	3.04	14.57	−3.47	1.23	3.63	4.70	3.52
	Pessimistic	−8.99	14.34	8.30	3.26	17.66	−3.18	1.29	3.60	4.20	4.22
Invest 2	Optimistic	−2.91	10.40	10.50	8.36	17.34	6.94	9.58	10.48	6.60	10.89
	Benchmark	−5.31	15.14	13.00	9.63	19.04	1.63	6.31	8.53	8.13	8.41
	Pessimistic	−7.26	15.59	14.18	11.34	23.11	2.34	6.15	7.68	8.49	9.14
Invest 3	Optimistic	−1.44	11.46	9.41	9.72	15.80	7.34	10.86	11.13	7.28	11.16
	Benchmark	−4.56	18.91	12.71	11.59	18.79	0.29	6.99	8.55	9.64	8.16
	Pessimistic	−6.04	21.86	15.34	13.96	22.83	−0.42	6.27	7.89	11.26	8.37
Invest 4	Optimistic	−3.91	10.02	10.54	7.95	18.33	6.69	8.79	10.09	6.18	10.72
	Benchmark	−5.86	13.11	12.51	8.86	19.20	2.50	5.89	8.51	7.19	8.57
	Pessimistic	−8.09	12.02	12.79	10.19	23.29	4.19	6.08	7.55	6.78	9.63

Note Invest 1 indicates fixed asset formation, Invest 2 indicates fixed assets investment (excluding farmers); Invest 3 indicates investment in state-owned and state-holding enterprises, and Invest 4 indicates investment in non-state-owned enterprises. *Source* CQMM team calculations

pandemic in the first half of the year will slow down the growth of investment, but the introduction of hedging policies can ease the degree of investment slowdown and maintain the stable growth of investment. The forecast results are as follows.

Under the optimistic scenario, the fixed asset investment (excluding farmers) calculated at current price will grow at 6.60% in 2020, up 1.17 percentage points higher over the previous year; in 2021, if China and the US can withdraw punitive tariffs in the first quarter, then fixed asset investment will increase by 10.89% (Table 2.1).

In term of quarters, in the first quarter of 2020, the growth rate of investment in fixed assets will −2.91% due to the impact of the COVID-19 pandemic and the delay of the resumption of work, production, and business activities; with the control of the COVID-19 pandemic, the growth rate of investment in the remaining three quarters will rise, reaching 10.40, 10.50 and 8.36% respectively. In the first quarter of 2021, due to the base effect, the investment growth rate may reach 17.34%, and the rest three quarters are expected to maintain more than double-digit growth level (see Fig. 2.5).

In terms of ownerships, in 2020, the investment of state-owned and state-holding enterprises is expected to increase by 7.28%, up 0.62 percentage points over the previous year. Among them, the growth rate of investment in the first quarter may decline to −1.44%. In 2020, non-state-owned investment will grow by 6.18%, up 1.49 percentage points; among them, the growth rate of investment in the first quarter will drop to −3.91%. In 2021, base effect plus the impact of expansion of the global trade, state-owned and state-holding investment will increase by 11.16%, and non-state-owned investment is expected to increase by 10.72% (Table 2.1).

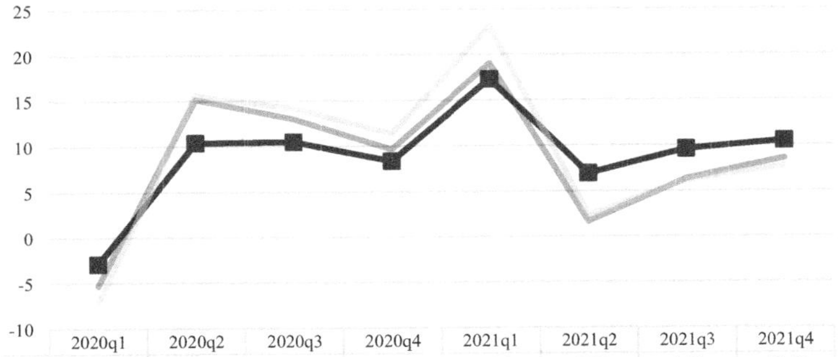

	2020q1	2020q2	2020q3	2020q4	2021q1	2021q2	2021q3	2021q4
FAI_SA	-2.91	10.40	10.50	8.36	17.34	6.94	9.58	10.48
Risk scenario 1	-5.31	15.14	13.00	9.63	19.04	1.63	6.31	8.53
Risk scenario 2	-7.26	15.59	14.18	11.34	23.11	2.34	6.15	7.68

Fig. 2.5 Projected growth rates of fixed asset investment. *Note* Risk scenario 1 and Risk scenario 2 refer to Benchmark and pessimistic scenario. *Source* CQMM team calculations

Under the Benchmark scenario, in the first quarter of 2020, the fixed asset investment may shrink by 5.31%. Among them, the investment of state-owned and state-holding enterprises may drop by 4.56% and that of non-state-owned enterprises may drop by 5.86%, indicating that the impact of the COVID-19 pandemic on the investment of non-state-owned enterprises is much greater. In the whole year, the investment in fixed assets will increase by 8.13%, up 2.69 percentage points over the previous year. Among them, the investment of state-owned and state-holding enterprises and non-state-owned enterprises will grow by 9.64 and 7.19%, up 2.99 and 2.50 percentage points respectively.

Under the pessimistic scenario, in the first quarter of 2020, the investment growth rate will decline more significantly (Table 2.1).

The above forecasts show that in 2020, although the impact of the COVID-19 pandemic in the first half of the year will slow down the growth of investment, a stronger hedging policy can slow down the decline of investment growth and keep it stable. The impact of the first quarter COVID-19 pandemic on the investment of non-state-owned enterprises is greater than the impact on the investment of state-owned and state-holding enterprises. Therefore, after the COVID-19 pandemic is completely controlled, China need to continue to ensure the implementation of policies and measures, such as financial services for the real economy, stable manufacturing investment and so on.

2.3.3 The Growth Rate of Residential Income and Consumption

In the first quarter of 2020, the impact of the COVID-19 pandemic significantly reduced the growth of consumption. Although consumption can rebound in the next three quarters, the annual consumption growth rate will fall slightly. The forecast results are as follow.

Under the optimistic scenario, the growth rate of consumption of residents will increase to 4.47% in 2020, a decrease of 2.17 percentage points over the previous year; it will increase to 7.65% in 2021. The growth rate of total retail sales of social consumption goods will be 7.58%, down 0.45 percentage points, and it can maintain 9.08% in 2021.

Under the Benchmark scenario, the growth rate of total retail sales of social consumption goods may decline to 5.79%. Under the pessimistic scenario, it may further fall to 4.48%.

In term of quarters, in the first quarter of 2020, not only part of the consumption demand of the Spring Festival was directly "evaporated" due to COVID-19 pandemic, but also the need to control the COVID-19 pandemic continues to restrain the consumption for a period of time. The total retail sale of social goods will fall by 0.14, 10.04 and 11.07% under the optimistic, Benchmark and pessimistic scenario, respectively. In the remaining quarters, the total retail sales of consumer goods will grow fast due to the rising prices. In addition, the base effect will lead to a significant rebound in the first quarter of 2021 (see Fig. 2.6).

Under the optimistic scenario, the per capita real disposable income of urban residents is expected to increase by 4.42%, down 0.54 percentage points over the previous year, and it will rise to 5.82% in 2021. The per capita cash income of rural

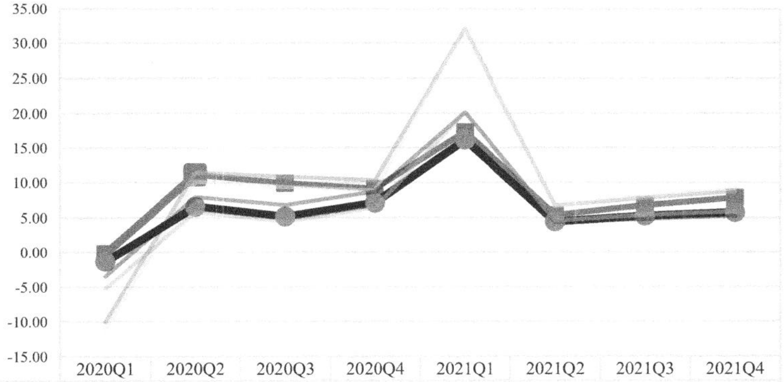

	2020Q1	2020Q2	2020Q3	2020Q4	2021Q1	2021Q2	2021Q3	2021Q4
RETAIL_SA	-0.14	11.15	9.93	9.13	17.36	5.39	6.79	7.82
Risk scenario 1	-10.04	11.45	10.84	10.32	32.08	6.68	7.78	8.75
Risk scenario 2	-11.07	10.17	9.37	8.86	31.97	6.65	8.04	9.14
CON_D_C_SA	-1.32	6.61	5.17	7.11	16.16	4.44	5.28	5.79
Risk scenario 1	-3.46	7.93	6.77	8.70	20.14	4.37	4.81	5.27
Risk scenario 2	-5.25	5.81	4.39	6.40	20.12	4.58	5.43	5.93

Fig. 2.6 Projected consumption growth. *Note* CON_D_C_SA represents the growth rate of total consumption in real term; RETAIL_SA indicates the growth rate of total retail sales in real term of social consumption goods; Risk scenario and Risk scenario 2 are benchmark and pessimistic respectively. *Source* CQMM team calculations

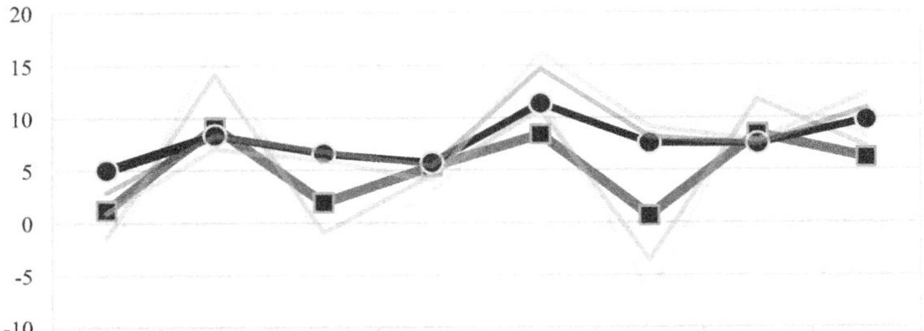

	2020Q1	2020Q2	2020Q3	2020Q4	2021Q1	2021Q2	2021Q3	2021Q4
YD_U_C_PC	1.22	9.16	1.91	5.36	8.41	0.66	8.45	6.15
Risk scenario 1	-1.39	14.16	-0.97	4.54	10.76	-3.58	11.73	7.20
Risk scenario 2	-3.62	17.31	-2.44	2.93	12.08	-6.85	12.64	8.22
YC_R_C_PC	5.03	8.38	6.60	5.74	11.39	7.59	7.52	9.81
Risk scenario 1	2.89	8.33	6.82	5.40	14.67	8.19	7.48	10.90
Risk scenario 2	1.00	7.04	5.91	4.02	16.25	9.13	7.82	12.31

Fig. 2.7 Projected income of the residents. *Note* YD_U_C_PC represents the real disposable income per capita of urban residents, YC_R_C_PC represents per capita cash income of rural residents. *Source* CQMM team assumptions

residents will increase by 6.44%, down 3.43 percentage points, and it will rise to 9.05% in 2021 (see Fig. 2.7).

Under the benchmark and pessimistic scenario, in 2020, the per capita disposable income of urban residents will increase by 4.09 and 3.55%, down 0.87 and 1.41 percentage points respectively; the per capita cash income of rural residents will increase by 5.87 and 4.51%, down 4.0 and 5.36 percentage points respectively.

Overall, in the next two years, the growth rate of the income and consumption of residents will continue to slow down.

2.3.4 The Growth Rates of Other Key Variables

(1) **The price indexes**

Under the optimistic scenario, in the first quarter of 2020, the impact of the COVID-19 pandemic on the supply, the rigid demand for essential goods and services, and the high pork prices will produce greater pressure on CPI. CPI may rise by 3.27% in 2020, up 0.37 percentage points higher over the previous year, and exceed the policy target of 3%; in 2021, the base effect may bring CPI down to 0.35%. In each of the four quarters of 2020, CPI will be 5.09, 4.43, 2.96 and 0.71%, compared with the same quarter of the previous year, respectively (see Fig. 2.8). Under the benchmark and pessimistic scenario, CPI growth in 2020 is likely to remain at 3.21–3.33%. The main pressure on CPI growth in the first half of 2020 comes from the rise of food CPI. Although the impact of the COVID-19 pandemic and the rise of pork prices are short-term, the impact of the sharp rise of CPI on the real income of urban and rural

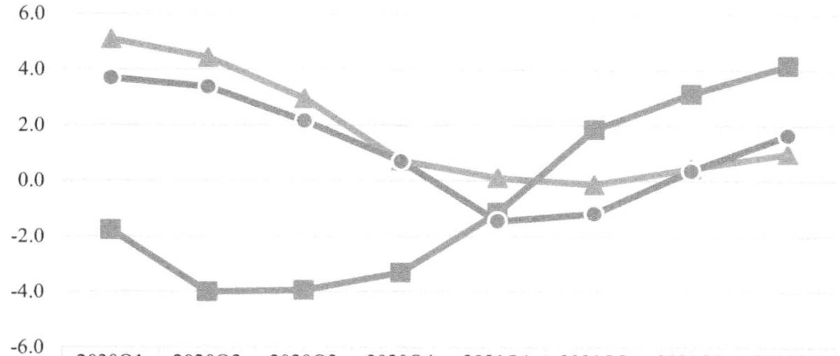

	2020Q1	2020Q2	2020Q3	2020Q4	2021Q1	2021Q2	2021Q3	2021Q4
CPI_SA	5.09	4.43	2.96	0.71	0.10	-0.13	0.45	0.98
PPI_SA	-1.75	-4.01	-3.95	-3.30	-1.13	1.86	3.15	4.17
PGDP_SA	3.70	3.38	2.16	0.70	-1.43	-1.17	0.37	1.66

Fig. 2.8 Projectedprice index. *Note* CPI_SA, PGDP_SA and PPI_ SA represents the seasonally adjusted consumer price index, GDP deflator and producer price index respectively. *Source* CQMM team calculations

residents, especially on the fixed income and low-income residents, needs to be paid enough attention.

Under the optimistic scenario, PPI will be −3.25 and 2.00% in 2020 and 2021. In the all quarters of 2020 and the first quarter of 2021, PPI will probably maintain negative growth, and the lowest point may appear in the second quarter of 2020 (see Fig. 2.8). Under the benchmark and pessimistic scenario, the impact of the COVID-19 pandemic on the domestic industrial chain from the demand side to the supply side has made PPI shrink in a larger extent in a longer period of time.

Under the optimistic scenario, the GDP deflator will increase by 2.30% in 2020, 0.74 percentage points lower than that in 2019, and fall by 0.13% in 2021. On a quarterly basis, the overall trend of its growth is from strong to weak, similar to that of the consumer price index (see Fig. 2.8). Under the benchmark and pessimistic scenarios, the GDP deflator will increase correspondingly.

(2) **The imports and exports**

In January 2020, China and the US successfully signed the first phase of trade agreement, which laid a good foundation for the two sides to ease and eventually eliminate trade friction. However, the outbreak of COVID-19 pandemic in the first half of the year will have a negative impact on global trade in the short term.

Under the optimistic scenario, Chinese total exports of goods will increase by 4.45% in 2020, up 4.59 percentage points over the previous year; the total imports of goods will increase by 6.33%, up 9.40 percentage points. In 2021, total exports and imports of goods will increase by 14.30 and 15.55% respectively (Table 2.2). Under the benchmark and pessimistic scenarios, in 2020, the total exports of goods will increase by 2.58 and 2.28%, up 2.72 and 2.42 percentage points respectively.

Table 2.2 Projected growth rates of imports and exports with the major trading partners from 2020 to 2021: %

Year	Trade partner	Exports				Imports			
		Current US$		Current RMB		Current US$		Current RMB	
		Optimistic	Pessimistic	Optimistic	Pessimistic	Optimistic	Pessimistic	Optimistic	Pessimistic
2020	Total	4.45	2.28	4.52	2.31	6.33	11.73	6.33	11.73
	US	−8.79	−9.41	−8.62	−9.26	10.64	10.40	10.54	10.09
	EU	6.48	5.48	6.55	5.54	10.93	8.68	10.97	8.72
	ASEAN	18.40	18.04	18.35	17.99	4.64	4.35	4.53	4.00
	The rest	4.15	3.37	4.21	3.42	5.32	5.23	5.35	5.17
2021	Total	14.30	16.52	11.73	13.93	15.55	10.08	12.99	7.65
	US	14.99	15.62	12.36	12.98	19.35	21.52	16.80	19.15
	EU	12.62	12.92	10.10	10.40	18.32	20.08	15.69	17.41
	ASEAN	21.22	21.32	18.51	18.61	13.67	15.35	11.23	13.14
	The rest	12.49	13.31	9.96	10.77	14.99	14.95	12.43	12.48

Source CQMM team calculations

The total imports of goods will increase by 11.76 and 11.73%, up 14.83 and 14.79 percentage points respectively.

In terms of countries, although China and the US successfully reached a trade agreement in January 2020, the US still will retain more projects and higher tariffs on Chinese exports, so Chinese exports to the US are likely to continue to shrink. On the other hand, Chinese import from the US will recover slightly due to the tax reduction.

In 2020, Chinese exports to the US will shrink by 8.79% in current dollar, an increase of 3.77 percentage points over the previous year; Chinese imports from the US will increase by 10.64%, an increase of 31.99 percentage points.

In 2020, Chinese exports to the EU will increase by 6.48%, up 2.4 percentage points; Chinese imports from the EU will increase by 10.93%, up 9.84 percentage points. In 2020, Chinese exports to ASEAN will increase by 18.40%, up 6.66 percentage points. Chinese imports from ASEAN will increase by 4.64%, up 0.44 percentage points.

In 2021, if China and the US can remove all punitive tariffs, then Chinese export share to the US will probably stabilize and increase.

Under the pessimistic scenario, in 2020, the growth rate of Chinese total exports may decline to 2.28% in current dollar terms, while the growth rate of total imports will remain at 10.40%.

To sum up, in the next two years, although the downward pressure still exists, some of the downward risks are expected to weaken. In particular, the Chinese government is promoting the transformation of economic structure and enhancing the resilience of the economy to resist downside risks. In terms of the monetary policies, based on the fundamental requirements of financial services for the real economy, the monetary policies adhere to the "stable" tone, while reforming the formation mechanism of the quoted interest rate (LPR) in the loan market through market-oriented reform. The LPR reform with its gradual effects can not only reduce the interest rate of enterprise loans, but also improve the efficiency of market allocation of credit resources, promote the effective adjustment of Chinese investment structure, and improve investment efficiency.

In terms of fiscal policies, with greater reduction of tax and fee, the burden of enterprises has been effectively reduced and the vitality of micro businesses has been enhanced; more importantly, various improvement measures to stabilize the investment in manufacturing industry have ensured the rapid growth of new energy investment, and the investment in the weak areas has been continuously developing and the investment structure has been gradually optimized.

The outbreak of COVID-19 pandemic in China and abroad will inevitably impact on the growth of China and the world economy in the first half of 2020. For the convenience of the readers, the above forecast results are summarized as follows.

1. **The GDP growth rate in 2020 and 2021**. In 2020, under optimistic, benchmark and pessimistic scenarios, GDP will grow by 5.09, 4.59 and 3.18%, respectively, 1.06, 1.55 and 2.96 percentage points lower than that in 2019. In the first quarter, GDP will grow at 0.94, −3.81 and −7.74%, under each of the three scenarios

respectively, compared with the same quarter of the previous year; In the second quarter, some economic activities suppressed in the early stage will be released gradually. GDP growth will rebound to 7.37–8.81%; the growth rate in the third and fourth quarters will be more stable. It will be in the intervals of 6.08–6.69% and 5.86–6.84%, because of the implementation of a series of more powerful monetary and fiscal hedging policies. In 2021, under the influence of base effect, GDP growth will rebound to 6.61–8.24%.

2. **The growth rate of investment in 2020 and 2021**. In 2020, the fixed asset investment (excluding farmers) calculated at current price is expected to grow at 6.60–8.49%, and the investment will grow slowly. In the first quarter, the fixed asset investment will grow at −2.91 to −7.26% compared with the same period of the previous year. In terms of ownership, the investment of state-owned and state-holding enterprises will grow at 7.28 to −11.26% and the investment of non-state-owned enterprises will grow at 6.18–7.18% in 2020. In the first quarter, the investment growth rate of state-owned and state-holding enterprises will be at −1.44 to −6.04%; the investment growth rate of non-state-owned enterprises will be at −3.91 to −8.09%. It shows that the impact of the first quarter COVID-19 pandemic on the non-state-owned enterprises is greater than the impact on the state-owned and state-holding enterprises. Therefore, after the COVID-19 pandemic has been completely controlled, it is necessary to continue implementing the relevant policies such as financial services for the real economy, stable manufacturing investment and so on. In 2021, investment growth is expected to be 8.41–10.89%.
3. **CPI**. In 2020, with the impact of the COVID-19 pandemic and pork prices, the CPI will to vary among the interval of 3.21–3.33%, exceeding the policy target of 3%. The CPI will be 5.09–5.24, 4.42–4.58, 2.84–2.99 and 0.52–0.71% in each of the four quarters, respectively. Although there is no basis for inflation or deflation, the sharp rise of CPI in the first half of the year will erode the real income of residents, especially of the low-income residents. In 2021, the base effect may make CPI increase to 0.27–0.38%.
4. **PPI**. In 2020, PPI will continue to shrink to 3.01–3.54%, hitting the lowest point in the second quarter. The impact of the COVID-19 pandemic on the domestic industrial chain, together with the sharp fluctuations in oil prices, will make PPI shrink in a longer period. In 2021, PPI may turn positive, increasing to 1.39–2.00%.
5. **The growth of residential income**. The nominal growth rate of total retail sales of social consumption goods may vary among the interval of 4.48–7.58% in 2020, and it is likely to drop sharply to −11.07 to −0.14% in the first quarter. In 2020, the growth rate of per capita real disposable income will be 3.55–4.42 and 4.51–6.44% for urban residents and rural residents respectively. The impact of the COVID-19 pandemic and the high price of pork will erode the real income growth of rural residents, especially of the low-income residents. The policy focus in 2020 should be to stabilize and improve the real income growth of rural residents and low-income residents. In 2021, the nominal growth rate of total retail sales of social consumption goods may rise to 9.08–12.92%.

6. **Exports and imports**. In 2020, the growth rate of Chinese total exports of goods will remain at 2.28–4.45%; the growth rate of total import of goods will be 6.33–11.76%. Among them, Chinese export growth rate to the US will drop to 8.79–9.41%; Chinese import growth rate from the US will be 10.64–11.73%. Chinese export growth to the EU will be 5.48–6.48%; Chinese import growth from the EU will be 8.68–10.93%. Chinese export growth to ASEAN will be 18.04–18.45%; Chinese import growth from ASEAN will be 4.35–4.64%. In 2021, the growth rate of Chinese total export of goods will increase to 14.30–16.52%; the growth rate of total import of goods will be 10.08–15.55%.

To sum up, Chinese economic growth will slow down in 2020. The impact of the COVID-19 pandemic combined with the high pork price, the annual CPI may exceed the policy target of 3%; the impact of the COVID-19 pandemic on the investment growth of non-state-owned enterprises is greater than that of state-owned enterprises and state-holding enterprises; the impact on the actual income of rural residents is greater than that of urban residents; the trend of stable and slow consumption growth throughout the year will continue. However, the impact of the COVID-19 pandemic is short-term and external. By increasing the hedging of macro policies and stimulating the vitality of micro businesses, the losses caused by the COVID-19 pandemic can be minimized, and Chinese economy can still maintain a stable and healthy development trend.

Chapter 3
The Policy Effects in Responding to COVID-19

In 2019, the weakening of global trade expansion and the escalation of trade frictions between China and the US have restrained the growth of private investment in Chinese manufacturing industry, and the decline in investment growth has become the main pressure on economic growth. The gross domestic product (GDP) grew by 6.1% in real terms, a decline of 0.6 percentage points over the previous year.

In 2020, the signing of the first phase of the economic and trade agreement between China and the US laid a good foundation for the two sides to ease and eventually eliminate trade frictions. At the same time, the implementation of loose monetary policies in many countries is likely to lead to the rebound of global trade, and is expected to drive the investment growth in Chinese export-oriented private manufacturing industry. The outbreak of COVID-19 pandemic in the first quarter, however, has inevitably affected the growth of Chinese economy and the global economy.

2020 is the key year of Chinese building a moderately prosperous society in an all respects and the end year of the 13th five-year plan, the last year of the "three major battles" against poverty, pollution, and potential risk. In the long run, the trend of Chinese economic stability to be good has not changed. However, in the short run, the downward pressure on the economy is still large.

In 2019, in order to cope with the downward pressure of economy, the Chinese government strengthened and improved macro-control. While continuing to implement prudent monetary policies, the financial policy increased efforts to promote tax reduction and fee reduction. Through a series of policy and measures such as improving the business environment and supporting the development of the real economy, China promoted the adjustment of investment structure and improved investment efficiency, ensuring the overall stable operation of the national economy. The improvement of development quality has laid a solid foundation for building a moderately prosperous society in all respects by 2020. However, the impact of the COVID-19 pandemic has brought greater challenges to concentrate on ensuring stability on the six fronts and security in the six areas.

China's Macroeconomic Outlook, Current Chinese Economic Report Series,
https://doi.org/10.1007/978-981-15-9279-9_3

In order to achieve the goal of "doubling the GDP and doubling the per capita income of residents compared with 2010" put forward by the Party, the GDP growth rate in 2020 must reach a targeted value of **5.62%**.[1] The growth rate of the GDP must be not less than 5.62% in 2020, but the predicted value is less than 5.62%. Based on this, if the policy focus of the first quarter is to boost the resumption of work, production, and business activities, expand production capacity, and ensure that the COVID-19 pandemic is fully controlled, then, in the rest of the year, coordination of monetary and fiscal policies are needed to stabilize economic growth.

Our research team believes that in terms of the monetary policies, China should continue to strengthen the fundamental requirements of financial services for the real economy, to deepen the structural reform of the financial supply side, to dredge the transmission of the monetary policies, and to improve the transmission efficiency of the monetary policies. In 2020, it is an important part of deepening the reform of interest rate marketization to improve the formation mechanism of the loan prime rate (LPR). From the perspective of supply side, the LPR reform with the reduction of the interest rate of loan for the enterprises, not only help to improve the efficiency of market allocation of credit resources, but also promote the adjustment of investment structure and improve investment efficiency; from the perspective of demand side, the LPR reform will help to reduce the interest burden of residential housing stock loans, and then increase the income and consumption of residents. In terms of the fiscal policies, it is necessary to increase the incentive of the demand side to the residential sector, and stabilize the income growth of residents, especially the income growth of rural residents, through tax reduction, expansion of transfer income to residents and stabilization of the employment market. Therefore, it is necessary to make full use of government bonds and all kinds of expenditure tools, appropriately increase the ratio of fiscal deficit to GDP. With a combination of the monetary and the fiscal policies, it is expected that in 2020, while stabilizing growth and achieving the goal of doubling, China will vigorously promote economic restructuring and improve growth efficiency.

Based on the above analysis, our research team analyze the effects on macro economy of the LPR reform and the fiscal expenditure expansion.

3.1 Background

The People's Bank of China (PBOC) started an interest rate reform on Aug 20, 2019, which we regard as a pragmatic start to unifying the "dual tracks" of interest rates—one for rates in the money market and the other for lending rates. Under the

[1]In 2010, China's GDP was about 41.21 trillion yuan. To achieve the goal of doubling the GDP, the GDP calculated at 2010 prices will reach 82.42 trillion yuan in 2020. Using the published annual real growth rates of GDP after 2010 (9.6, 7.9, 7.8, 7.4, 7.0, 6.8, 6.9, 6.7 and 6.1%, respectively), we can get a GDP of about 78.04 trillion yuan calculated at 2010 prices in 2019. Then, in order to achieve the goal of doubling, it is necessary to maintain the real growth rate of GDP at 5.62% or above in 2020.

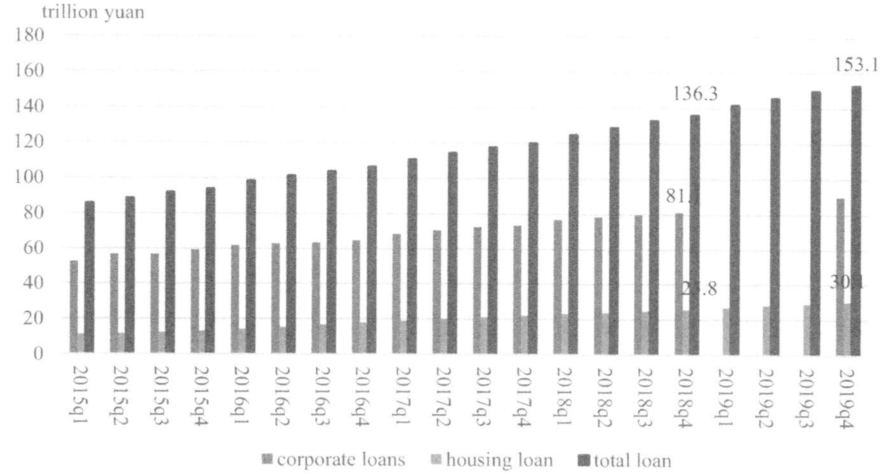

Fig. 3.1 Total loans by category of financial institutions. *Source* CQMM team calculations

reform, the PBOC has improved the formation mechanism of the loan prime rate (LPR)—the price of loans banks offer their best clients—and use the LPR as the reference rate for business and household loans. The earlier reference rate, the one-year benchmark lending rate, will be replaced in the future. As the start in interest rate unification, the reform can help ease the financing woes faced by small and medium-sized enterprises (SMEs), act as a prelude to more interest rate reforms, and give clues to China's macro policy-setting pattern. The reform served as a timely measure to tackle such economic downward pressure, especially considering that traditional monetary policy tools have limited wriggle room as inflation pressure and macro leverage stay high.

Statistics show that as of the fourth quarter of 2019, the total loans of Chinese financial institutions was about 153.1 trillion yuan. Among them, the total amount of personal housing loans was about 30.1 trillion yuan, accounting for about 19.6% of the total loans, an increase of 0.7 percentage points over the same period in 2018; the total amount of corporate loans was about 90.0 trillion yuan (see Fig. 3.1).[2]

With the promotion of the LPR reform, the interest rate of outstanding loans of enterprises as well as residents would be reduced (see Fig. 3.2).

[2]Due to the lack of data on the total amount of corporate loans, here, we make the following calculation: using the proportion of corporate loans in the total loans in the fourth quarter of 2018 (59.5%), considering the increase in the proportion of personal housing loans (0.7%), to estimate that the total amount of corporate loans in the fourth quarter of 2019 is about 90.0 trillion yuan.

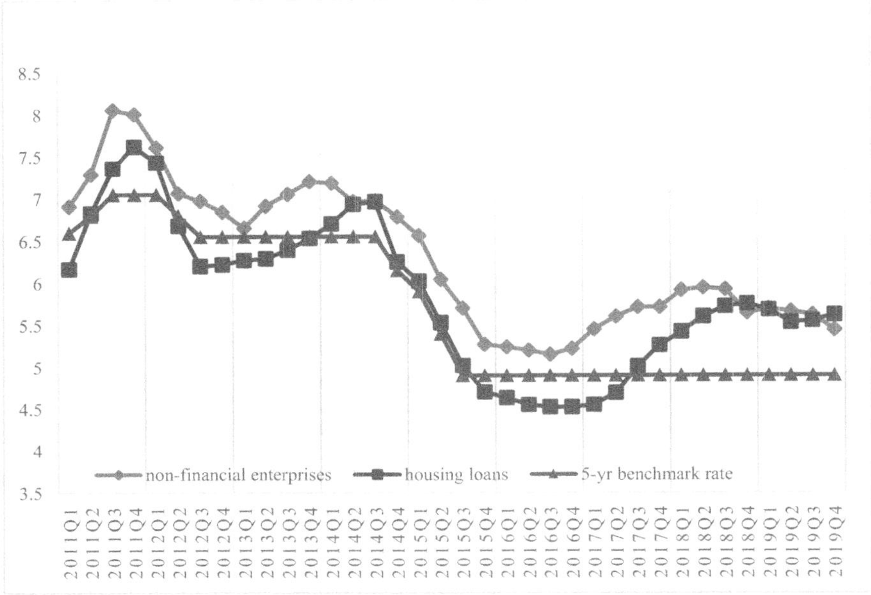

Fig. 3.2 The comparison between interest rate and benchmark interest. *Source* CQMM team calculations

3.2 Scenario Design to Simulate Policy Effect

In order to analyze the effect on macroeconomy of the policy combination of LPR reform and fiscal expenditure expansion, our research team designed two simulation scenarios to simulate the macroeconomic effects.

Defining the benchmark scenario: with the reform of LPR but without further expansion of fiscal expenditure. It is assumed that the one-year and five-year LPR interest rates at the end of 2020 will drop **20 basis points** compared with the end of 2019, reaching 3.85 and 4.55% at the end of the 2020, and keep unchanged to the end of 2021. At the same time, the growth rate of fiscal expenditure in this year and next will maintain the same level of 2019, reaching 8.2%. Under this benchmark scenario, compared with the old interest rate mechanism, the interest expense of enterprise is expected to decrease by 90, 135, 185 and 225 billion yuan respectively in the each of the four quarters of 2020; the interest burden of enterprises can be further reduced in each quarter of 2021. On the other hand, in 2020, the interest burden of residents can be reduced by 75.25 billion yuan in each quarter of 2021.

Defining the simulation scenario 1: without the reform of LPR and without further expansion of fiscal expenditure. Assuming that LPR reform has not been promoted by the end of 2019, the old interest rate mechanism based on RMB basic loan interest rate is still maintained. Compared with the benchmark scenario, the interest burden of enterprises and residents is relatively heavier. With the comparison between the scenario 1 and the benchmark scenario, we can depict the effects of promoting LPR reform.

Defining the simulation scenario 2: with the reform of LPR as well as with further expansion of fiscal expenditure. As in the benchmark scenario, assuming LPR reform, the interest rate will be reduced by **20 basis points**. In order to keep the GDP growth rate at 5.62% in 2020, then the growth rate of fiscal expenditure increase to 15.8%

In addition, on the basis of simulation scenario 2, to analyzes the substitution effect and structural change effect between interest rate reduction and fiscal expenditure growth, our research team also assumes that the one-year and five-year LPR interest rates at the end of 2020 will drop **60 instead of 20 basis points** compared with the end of 2019. Then, under the premise of maintaining GDP growth rate of 5.62%, with a greater interest rate cut, we can analyze the substitution effect between interest rate reduction and fiscal expenditure expansion.

3.3 Analysis of the Impact of Policy Simulation

3.3.1 The Effect on Macro Economy of LPR Reform

First, the LPR reform with a reduction of market interest rate will help to increase the growth rate of GDP. Compared with the simulation scenario 1, the LPR reform under the benchmark scenario will increase GDP growth by 0.27 and 1.12 percentage points respectively in 2020 and 2021 (see Fig. 3.3). It shows that the reduction of market interest rate has obvious incentive effect on economic growth. However, the effect

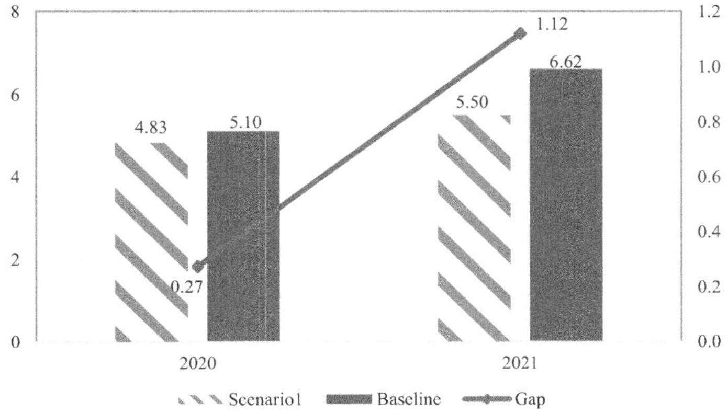

Fig. 3.3 The growth rate of GDP. *Note* Baseline represents the benchmark scenario. *Source* CQMM team calculations

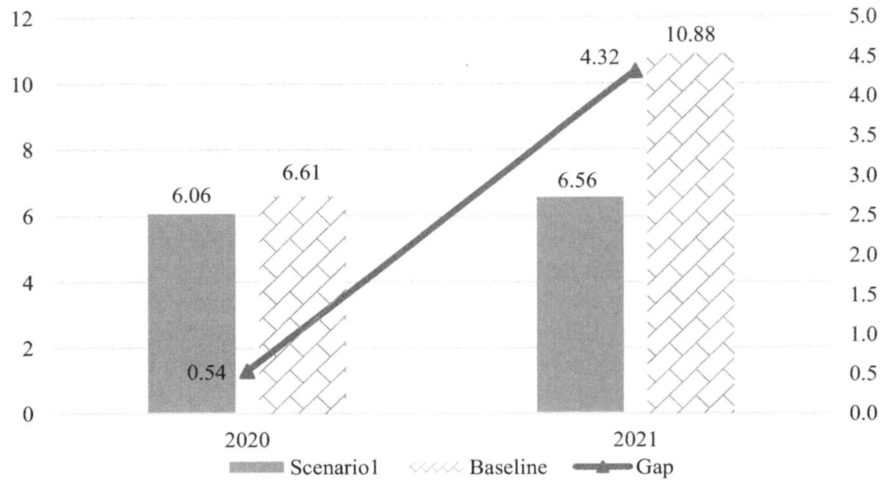

Fig. 3.4 The growth rate of urban fixed asset investment. *Note* Baseline represents the benchmark scenario. *Source* CQMM team calculations

is weaker in 2020 compared with in 2021. Therefore, the earlier the LPR reform is carried out, the better the recovery of economic growth will be.

Secondly, the LPR reform with a reduction of market interest rate has an obvious incentive effect on the growth of investment, especially private investment. Compared with the simulation scenario 1, the growth rate of urban fixed asset investment under the benchmark scenario can be increased by 0.54 and 4.32 percentage points respectively in 2020 and 2021 (see Fig. 3.4); among them, the growth rate of private investment can be increased by 1.55 and 9.06 percentage points respectively (see Fig. 3.5). The LPR reform has three channels to stimulate investment: first, the "price effect", which directly reduces the financing cost of enterprises, especially private enterprises, and encourages them to expand investment; second, the "cost effect" of enterprises, which reduces the interest burden of enterprise; third, "cost effect" of residents, which reduces the interest burden of housing loans. Based on the simulation results, the private investment is more sensitive to the market interest rate.

Third, the growth rate of residential consumption increased slightly, which benefited from the acceleration of economic growth and the reduction of interest burden on housing loans. Under the benchmark scenario, the growth rate of resident consumption calculated by the comparable price can be increased by 0.02 and 0.16 percentage points respectively in 2020 and 2021 compared with the scenario 1 (see Fig. 3.6).

Finally, the acceleration of investment and consumption will increase the growth rate of imports and exports. Under the benchmark scenario, the export growth rate will increase by 0.01 and 0.1 percentage points respectively compared with the simulation

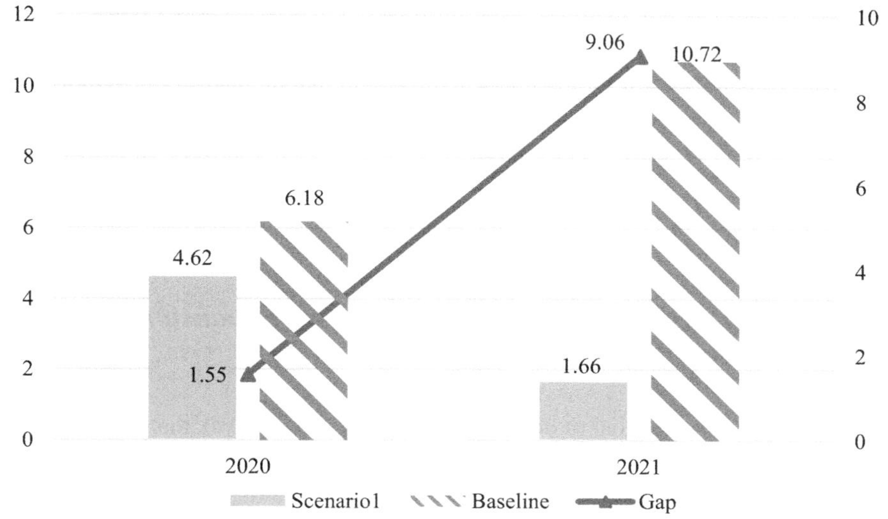

Fig. 3.5 The growth rate of private investment. *Note* Baseline represents the benchmark scenario. *Source* CQMM team calculations

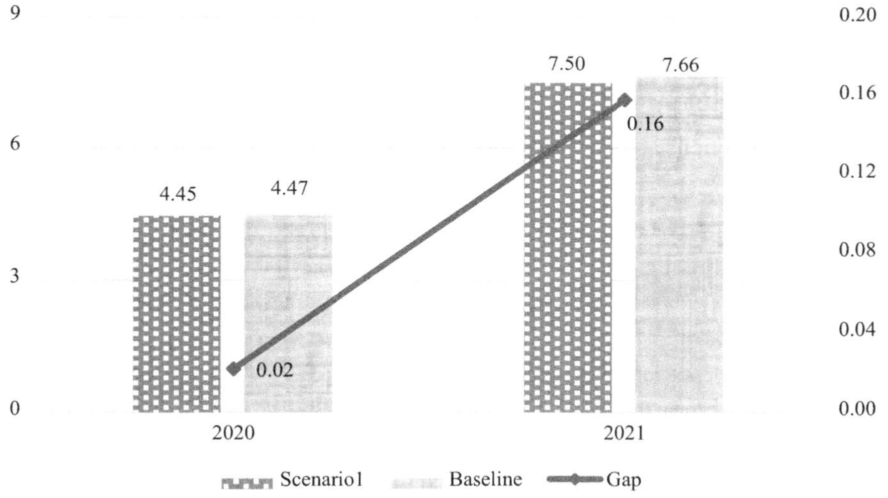

Fig. 3.6 The growth rate of residential consumption. *Note* Baseline represents the benchmark scenario. *Source* CQMM team calculations

scenario 1 in 2020 and 2021; the import growth rate can increase by 0.66 and 1.83 percentage points respectively in 2020 and 2021.

To sum up, the LPR reform with the reduction of market interest rate will help to increase economic growth, stimulate the investment growth of enterprises, especially private enterprises, and promote the growth of residential consumption and imports and exports. Due to time lag, the effect on economy in 2021 is stronger than that in 2020.

3.3.2 The Policy Effects of LPR Reform and Expansion of Fiscal Expenditure

In order to achieve the goal of doubling GDP in 2020 over 2010, the growth rate of the GDP must be not less than **5.62%** in 2020, but the predicted value is less than 5.62%. Although the Chinese government has issued and implemented a number of policies in the first quarter to boost the resumption of work, production, and business activities, and expand production capacity, it is still necessary to coordinate monetary and fiscal policies for the rest of the time after the COVID-19 pandemic is fully controlled.

To analyze the effects, our research team made two assumptions to increase GDP growth. **Assumption 1**: the market interest rate will fall by 20 basis points, and fiscal expenditure increase by 15.8%; **Assumption 2**, the market interest rate will fall by 60 basis points, and fiscal expenditure increase by 15.3%. The policy effects under the two assumptions are shown in Table 3.1.

Tabel 3.1 The effects of different policy combinations in 2020: %

Growth rate	Policy 1	Gap 1	Policy 2	Gap 2
Real GDP	5.62	0.53	5.62	0.53
Real consumption	4.52	0.05	4.52	0.05
Nominal retail sales of consumer goods	7.63	0.05	7.64	0.06
Real comparable capital formation	3.52	0.12	3.45	0.05
Nominal urban fixed asset investment	6.77	0.17	6.82	0.22
Investment of state-owned and state-holding enterprises	7.74	0.46	7.32	0.04
Private investment	6.19	0.01	6.56	0.38
Total export (current price, USD)	4.46	0.01	4.46	0.01
Total import (current price, USD)	7.33	1.00	7.32	1.00
Share of public expenditure in GDP	7.1		7.0	

Note Policy 1 is the policy combination of an LPR reform with a reduction of interest rate by 20 basis points and an increase of fiscal expenditure by 15.8%. Policy 2 is the policy combination of an LPR reform with a reduction of interest rate by 60 basis points and an increase of fiscal expenditure by 15.3%. Gap 1 is the between the policy 1 and the baseline, gap 2 is the between the policy 2 and the baseline. *Source* CQMM team calculations

Under the assumption 1, in order to achieve the targeted growth rate of GDP at 5.62%, additional fiscal expenditure of 1814.5 billion yuan should be added in 2020, increased by 15.8%. If the growth rate of fiscal revenue remains unchanged, the proportion of fiscal deficit in GDP has to increase to 7.1% in 2020, up 2.1 percentage points over the previous year.

Under assumption 2, in order to achieve the targeted growth rate of GDP at 5.62%, additional fiscal expenditure of 1719 billion yuan should be added in 2020.

Under the two assumptions, the difference of extra fiscal expenditure is small, which may be due to the fact that the economic stimulus effect of LPR reform with a reduction of the interest rate has a time lag, so the substitution effect between interest rate reduction and fiscal expansion is not obvious.

Under the assumption 1, with the reduction of the interest rate by 20 basis points, the growth rate of private investment can be increased to 6.19%, 0.01 percentage points higher than that of the benchmark scenario; Under the assumption 2, with the reduction of the interest rate by 60 basis points, the growth rate of private investment can be increased to 6.56%, 0.38 percentage points higher than that of the benchmark scenario. A bigger interest rate reduction has a significant effect on private investment in 2020, because private investment is more sensitive to interest rate. Besides, the expansion of fiscal expenditure can further improve the growth rate of private investment by reducing enterprise costs from the supply side, reducing residential tax burden from the demand side, and expanding the transfer income to residents so as to increase residential consumption.

By contrast, under the assumption 1, the investment growth rate of state-owned and state-holding enterprises is faster than that of the benchmark scenario. It shows that a larger interest rate reduction can not only stabilize economic growth, but also effectively stimulate the growth of private investment. This not only drives the recovery of investment growth (gross effect), but also promote the adjustment of investment structure and improve investment efficiency (structural effect).

Due to the timing of LPR reform, the interest rate of outstanding housing loans will not change in 2020. However, the acceleration of the growth of fiscal expenditure can promote the growth of residential consumption through such channels as the reduction of residential tax burden, the increase of transfer income of residents and the expansion of employment security expenditure. Compared with the benchmark scenario, the real growth rate of residential consumption can be increased by 0.05 percentage points, and the nominal growth rate of total retail sales of consumer goods can be increased by 0.05–0.06 percentage points.

Finally, thanks to the growth of private investment and the slight pick-up of consumption growth, in 2020, in terms of the current dollar price, the export growth rate remained stable, 0.01 percentage points higher than that under the benchmark scenario; the import growth rate is expected to increase by 1.0 percentage points.

In conclusion, the COVID-19 pandemic in the first quarter of 2020 will inevitably have a significant negative impact on Chinese economy. Even in the benchmark case, the GDP is expected to increase by 5.09% in 2020, which is 0.53 percentage points lower than the targeted growth rate of 5.62%. Although the Chinese government has issued and implemented a number of policies in the first quarter to boost the resumption of work, production, and business activities, and expand production capacity, it is still necessary to coordinate the monetary and fiscal policies throughout to stabilize economic growth. The main suggestions are as follows.

First, with the reduction of the interest rate by 20 basis points, and the increase of fiscal expenditure by 15.8%, the proportion of fiscal deficit in GDP will increase to 7.1% in 2020, assuming that the growth rate of fiscal revenue remains unchanged. Under the LPR reform with a reduction of the interest rate by 60 basis points, and the growth of fiscal expenditure by 15.3%, the proportion of fiscal deficit in GDP will increase to 7.0% in 2020, assuming that the growth rate of fiscal revenue remains unchanged.

Second, the implementation of different policy combinations not only improve economic growth (total expansion effect), but also improve investment structure and efficiency (structural adjustment effect). From the supply side, the LPR reform with a reduction of interest rate can effectively stimulate the growth (price effect) of private investment, which is more sensitive to the change of interest rate. At the same time, the reduction of interest burden will help to expand the investment (cost effect) of private enterprises. From the demand side, the reduction of market interest rate in 2020 can reduce the interest burden (cost effect) of the outstanding housing loans in 2021, thus strengthening the residential expectation on income growth. It is expected to stabilize the growth of the real income of residents by coordinating with the fiscal expenditure policies such as reducing the tax burden of residents, increasing the transfer income to residents and stabilizing the employment market, so as to drive the growth of the consumption of residents, and finally promote the growth of investment from the demand side. The policy combination can effectively stimulate the growth of private investment while stabilizing economic growth, and then promote the adjustment of investment structure and improve investment efficiency.

It should be noted that the results of the above policy effect simulation are subject to the model setup and the assumptions of exogenous variables. An important significance of policy simulation is that it can quantify the change direction of aggregate effect and structural effect, so as to provide a reference for policy decision-maker.

Chapter 4
Conclusions and Policy Recommendations

In 2019, the weakening of global trade expansion has restrained the growth of private investment in manufacturing industry in China; the growth of industrial profits declined significantly; and the downward pressure on economic growth has been increasing. The real GDP growth rate was 6.1%, 0.6 percentage points over the previous year.

First, the growth rate of fixed asset investment continued to decline. In 2019, the fixed asset investment (excluding farmers) increased 5.4%, down 0.5 percentage points over the previous year; the contribution rate of capital formation to GDP growth decreased to 31.2%, down 10.3 percentage points, the lowest in the past 20 years. Private investment increased 4.7%, down 4.0 percentage points. The private investment accounted for 56.4% in total investment, down 5.6 percentage points, the lowest level in the past decade.

Secondly, the expansion of industrial production slowed down, and the growth rate of industrial profits fell sharply. The value-added of enterprises above designated size in real term increased 5.7%, down 0.5 percentage points, which was the lowest growth rate in the past 20 years. The profit of enterprises above designated size has shrunk 3.3%, a drop of 13.6 percentage points, which was the biggest drop in the past five years.

Thirdly, the growth of residential income continued to slow down. The per capita real disposable income increased by 5.8%, down 0.7 percentage points over the previous year, the lowest growth rate in the past five years. The per capita real disposable income of urban residents and rural residents increased by 5.0 and 6.2%, down 0.6 and 0.4 percentage points respectively.

Finally, the growth rate of imports and exports of goods slowed down in 2019. The total export (RMB value) increased 5.0%, down 2.1 percentage points; the total import (RMB value) increased 1.6%, down 11.3 percentage points. The trade surplus reached 2918 billion yuan, increasing 593.29 billion yuan (see Fig. 1.12).

In order to cope with the downward pressure at home and from abroad, Chinese government changed the response policies and measures. Under the premise of preventing financial risks and controlling financial leverage, Chinese government

China's Macroeconomic Outlook, Current Chinese Economic Report Series,
https://doi.org/10.1007/978-981-15-9279-9_4

strengthened and improved macro-control, introduced a series of policies and measures, such as cutting taxes and fees, improving business environment, and supporting the development of the real economy. The economy showed a stable and progressive trend. In terms of the monetary policies, based on the fundamental requirements of financial services for the real economy, under the premise of ensuring sufficient liquidity, China increased the proportion of new RMB loans to the real economy; China promoted the reform of the formation mechanism of the loan prime rate (LPR), broke the lower limit of the interest rate in the loan market, effectively reduced the financing burden of enterprises, and improved the allocation efficiency of credit resources. Although the growth rate of fiscal revenue continues to decline, fiscal expenditure has been stable and the growth drivers have been strengthened; at the same time, taxes reduction and expansion of transfer income to residents have stabilized the growth of residential income. In addition, the sustained fiscal investment in the weak areas are also optimizing of the investment structure.

In 2020, the signing of the first phase of the trade agreement between China and the US laid a good foundation for the two sides to ease and eventually eliminate trade frictions. At the same time, the continued implementation of loose monetary policies in major countries is likely to lead to a rebound of global trade, and is expected to drive the growth of private investment in manufacturing industry in China. The outbreak of COVID-19 pandemic in the first quarter, however, has inevitably affected the growth of China and the world economy in 2020.

The predicted results based on CQMM model show that, in 2020, although the growth of global trade may rebound from the bottom and the expectation of smooth progress of China and the US trade negotiations and other positive factors are expected to stabilize and enhance the growth of Chinese fixed asset investment, the impact of the COVID-19 pandemic in the first quarter will slow down the growth of investment to a certain extent. In 2020, Chinese GDP growth may decline to 5.31%, down 0.83% points over 2019 under the optimistic scenario; the GDP growth is expected to further decline to 5.09% and to 4.77% under the benchmark and pessimistic scenario respectively. The impact of the COVID-19 pandemic on the investment growth of non-state-owned enterprises is greater than that of state-owned enterprises and state-holding enterprises; the impact on the real income of rural residents is greater than that of urban residents; with the high pork price, the rise of CPI will further weaken the income growth of low-income residents, thus inhibiting the growth of consumption.

2020 is the key year of China building a moderately prosperous society in all respects, the ending year of the 13th five-year plan, the last year and the "decisive year" of the "three critical battles". Though China economy to be stable and good in the long run, the downward pressure on the economy is still large in the short run.

In order to achieve the goal of "doubling the GDP and per capita income of urban and rural residents compared with 2010" put forward at the 18th National Congress, the growth rate of the GDP must be not less than 5.62% in 2020, but the predicted value is less than 5.62%. Based on this, if the policies in the first quarter focused on boosting the resumption of work, production, and business activities, expanding production capacity, and full controlling of the COVID-19 pandemic, then, for the rest of the year, coordination of monetary and fiscal policies are necessary to stabilize economic growth.

In 2020, it is an important part of deepening the reform of interest rate marketization in the loan market. From the perspective of the supply side, an LPR reform with a reduction of the interest rate can reduce the interest burden (cost effect) of enterprises. This will not only improve the efficiency of market allocation of credit resources, but also promote the adjustment of investment structure and improve investment efficiency. From the demand side, an LPR reform with a reduction of the interest rate will help to reduce the interest burden of housing loans, and then increase real income of residents. In the supply side, fiscal policies continue to cut taxes and fees, improve regulation and optimize services, and optimize business environment. In the demand side, it is necessary to increase the incentive in the residential sector, and stabilize the income growth of residents, especially of the rural residents, through tax reduction, expansion of transfer income to residents and stabilization of the employment market. Therefore, it is necessary to make full use of government bonds and all kinds of fiscal tools, appropriately increase the ratio of fiscal deficit to GDP; at the same time, activate the financial stock funds, and improve the efficiency of financial funds. With these combinations of monetary and fiscal policies, it is expected that in 2020, China will vigorously promote economic restructure and improve growth efficiency.

Based on the CQMM model, our research team analyzed the possible macroeconomic effects of different combinations of LPR reform and fiscal expenditure expansion. The results show that, with the LPR reform, if the growth rate of fiscal revenue in 2020 maintained the level of last year, 3.8%, the growth rate of fiscal expenditure may need to be increased from 8.2% in 2019 to 15.3 or 15.8% in 2020, and the share of fiscal deficit in GDP may increase to 7.0%, 2.1 percentage points higher than that in 2019. The reduction of interest rate can effectively stimulate the growth of private investment which is more sensitive to the interest rate; with the fiscal policies such as tax reduction, the growth of private investment is expected to increase further. From the perspective of the demand side, the reduction of the interest burden of the housing loan can strengthen the expectation of the growth of the residential income; under the fiscal policies such as reducing the tax burden, accelerating the transfer income to residents and stabilizing the employment market, it is expected to stabilize the growth of the real income of residents, thus driving the growth of the residential consumption, and finally promoting the growth of the investment. Different policy combinations can effectively stimulate the growth of private investment while stabilizing economic growth, and then improve the investment structure and investment efficiency.

Based on this, our research team proposed as follows.

First, GDP growth is expected to fall below 6% in 2020. Despite the signing of the first phase of economic and trade agreement between China and US, which has laid a good foundation for easing and eliminating trade frictions, but the outbreak of the COVID-19 pandemic in the first quarter has inevitably affected the growth of China and the global economy, and has increased the difficulty of achieving "doubling goal" of Chinese GDP in 2020 compared to 2010. In the face of the decline of economic growth, on the basis of the introduction of various policies to deal with the impact of COVID-19 pandemic in the first quarter, the policy authorities should continue to implement various policies and measures to prevent and control financial risks, to curb the expansion of the real estate industry and the local government debt; continue the control measures of the monetary and fiscal policies implemented in 2019, so as to ensure the adjustment of economic structure and stabilization of economic growth.

Second, China should continue to implement prudent monetary policies and prudential fiscal policy. In 2020, while making effort to do a good job in financial services, China should ensure that the share of loans to real economy is more than 60%, and truly implement the requirements of financial services for the real economy. China should implement and promote the reform of LPR, encourage the growth of private investment which is more sensitive to the interest rate, improve the efficiency of market allocation of credit resources, promote the adjustment of investment structure and improve the investment efficiency. China should further give full play to the structural guidance role of credit policies, ensure that funds are invested in advanced manufacturing, people's livelihood construction, infrastructure, and promote the "double upgrading" of industry and consumption. China should actively do a good job in financial support for employment and entrepreneurship, carry out poverty alleviation and continue to strengthen financial support for industrial upgrading.

Third, China should appropriately speed up the growth of fiscal expenditure and focus on stabilizing the real income growth of residents. China should make full and flexible use of government bonds and various expenditure tools, appropriately accelerate the growth of public financial expenditure, appropriately expand the deficit, especially the central fiscal deficit. The expansion of fiscal expenditure should focus on the people's livelihood, stabilize the real income of residents, especially the income growth of low-income residents, and promote the stable growth of consumption from the aspects of improving people's livelihood, social security, through measures such as reducing tax, increasing the transfer income to residents and ensuring the stability of the employment market. China should further optimize the way of tax and fee reduction, and shift from the current VAT reduction to the social security rates reduction and corporate income tax reduction. China should continue to push forward the investment in weak areas, such as new infrastructure construction.

Fourth, to stabilize investment, China should focus on the long-term goal of "improving the competitiveness of enterprises". After the COVID-19 pandemic has been completely controlled, it is necessary to continue to implement the policies such as financial services for the real economy, stable manufacturing investment and so on. However, the implementation of the policies should be able to squeeze out inefficient investment, promote the growth of effective investment and release the potential of domestic market demand; continue to deepen the reform of state-owned enterprises, implement competition neutrality and ownership neutrality, eliminate ownership discrimination, accelerate the construction of a fair competition business environment, improve the property rights protection system, expand the development space of private economy, boost the confidence of enterprises. China should continue to increase tax cutting for innovative enterprises and high-tech enterprises, encourage enterprises to expand R&D investment, enhance innovation ability, increase the share of high-tech manufacturing industry, accelerate industrial upgrading, then realize the sustained and rapid growth of labor productivity.

Fifth, China should pay more attention to the impact of the COVID-19 pandemic and the impact of high food CPI on the real income of residents, especially the low-income residents. Although the current economy does not have the basis of serious inflation, but in the first half of 2020, the impact of the COVID-19 pandemic and the high pork prices will keep CPI at a high level. Therefore, price stabilization is still a top priority. China should stabilize CPI on the basis of curbing the excessive rise of meat prices. China should continue to implement the policy of taxes and fees cutting, increase the transfer income to low-income residents, accelerate the transfer of part of state-owned capital to enrich social security fund, ensure the deduction of social security rate, and ensure the growth of real income of residents, especially low-income residents.

Sixth, China should guide the coordinated development of industrial transformation and employment promotion in order to achieve stable growth of employment, especially in high-income jobs. In recent years, with the continuous increase of wage level in China, the share of labor-intensive manufacturing industry has declined rapidly, which aggravates the conflict between the transformation of industrial structure and the promotion of employment; at the same time, the share of traditional service industry in the tertiary industry is relatively high, but most of it are with low-income jobs. Therefore, while stabilizing the total employment, China should improve the employment structure, improve the quality of employment, and ensure the stable growth of high-income jobs; while promoting the development of small and medium-sized enterprises (SMEs), China should give greater support to entrepreneurship and innovation activities, further strengthen vocational skills training, and accurately carry out the employment work of key group of residents.

Appendix A
Report on Questionnaire Survey on the Outlook for China's Economy and Policy

First time, January 2020

Second time, March 2020

No. 14

In order to grasp Chinese macroeconomic situation and policy trends in a timely manner, the Center for Macroeconomic Research at Xiamen University and the Economic Information Daily of Xinhua News Agency jointly carried out an annual questionnaire survey on the outlook for China's macroeconomy and policy since August 2013.

This is the 14th survey. The questionnaire designed 20 questions directly related to macroeconomic operation and policy trends in China, one before and the other after the outbreak of COVID-19 pandemic. In January and March 2020, we sent email invitations to economists. A valid response was received from 121 and 105 experts respectively. Through this questionnaire survey, we have obtained the latest professional understanding and expectations on the economic situation of China and the World, and the impact of the COVID-19 pandemic on Chinese macroeconomic policy trend in 2020. The results of this questionnaire are published as follows.

A.1 Questionnaire Survey I

January 20th–February 20th, 2020

Outlook for the World Economy in 2020

According to the forecast of the International Monetary Fund (IMF) on January 20th, 2020, of the Federal Reserve in December 2019, and of the World Bank in

China's Macroeconomic Outlook, Current Chinese Economic Report Series,
https://doi.org/10.1007/978-981-15-9279-9

January 2020, the economic growth of the US will slow down to 2.0, 2.0 and 1.8% in 2020 respectively. According to the survey results, 76% of the experts expect the US economic growth rate will be 1.6–2.0% in 2020; 17% experts expect between 2.1–2.5%; 7% experts expect below 1.5%. Overall, more than 80% of experts expect that the US economy will grow slower in 2020 than in 2019.

According to the forecast of the IMF on January 20, 2020, and the forecast of the World Bank in January 2020, the economic growth rate of the Euro zone will be 1.3% and 1.0% in 2020, respectively.

According to the survey results, 69% of the experts expect that the economic growth rate of the Eurozone will be 1.1–1.3% in 2020; 29% experts expect below 1.0%; 2 experts expect 1.4–1.6%. Overall, all the experts agreed that the economic growth rate of the Eurozone in 2020 will be lower than in 2019.

In 2019, the rise of trade protectionism restrained the growth of global trade, the export was sluggish, and the export order index fell below the threshold value of 50, and the growth of manufacturing investment slowed down. In 2020, the US economy will still face many challenges, including the impact of the trade friction between China and the US, the growth rate of private consumption expenditure in the U.S. may decline; on the other hand, The Brexit had effects on the economic growth of the Euro area and slowed down the German economy. At the end of 2019, the exchange rate of the Euro against the US dollar is 1.2, down 2.18% from the beginning of the year. By January 20th, 2020, the exchange rate is 1.1099, a decrease of 0.94% compared with the beginning of 2020. The survey results show that compared with 2019, 48% of the experts expect that the Euro will continue to depreciate against the US dollar in 2020. At the end of 2020, the exchange rate will be 1.0–1.125, with an average value of 1.0732.

According to the survey, 40% experts expect that the exchange rate will remain stable. 12% experts expect that it will appreciate in the end of 2020, which will be 1.1–1.2, with an average of 1.1396. Overall, nearly half of the experts believe that the Euro will continue to depreciate in 2020.

Influenced by the global economic slowdown, trade tensions and some uncertainties, the Federal Reserve cut interest rates three times in 2019 by a total of 75 basis points to provide "buffer" and "insurance" for the US economy. On December 11, 2019, the Federal Reserve ended its last monetary policy meeting of the year, announcing to keep the target range of the federal fund interest rate unchanged at 1.5–1.75%. What do you think is the possible position of US monetary policies by the end of 2020? The survey results show that 47% experts expect the Federal Reserve to start a long-term interest rate reduction cycle in 2020. Among them, 28% experts believe that the Federal Reserve will start a long-term interest rate reduction cycle once a year, 15% experts believe that the Federal Reserve will cut interest rates twice a year, 4% experts believe that the Federal Reserve will cut interest rates three times a year; 28% experts expect that there is uncertainty in the monetary policies of the Federal Reserve; 20% experts expect the Federal Reserve will not cut interest rates within the year; 3% experts believe that based on the performance of American economic data, the Federal Reserve will increase interest rates 1 or 2 times within the year to prevent the economy from overheating; 2% experts expect the Federal Reserve will cut interest rates 1–2 times within the year.

Outlook for China's Economy in 2020

According to the preliminary accounting data released by the National Bureau of Statistics on January 17, 2020, Chinese GDP grew 6.1% in 2019, down 0.5% over the previous year. From the quarterly view, the growth rates were 6.4, 6.2, 6.0 and 6.0% in the four quarters respectively. According to the forecast of the International Monetary Fund on January 20th, 2020, Chinese GDP will grow 6.0% in 2020.

With regard to Chinese GDP growth rate in 2020, 63% experts expect to be below 5.9%; 24% experts expect 5.9–6.0%; 8% experts expect 6.0–6.1%; 3% experts expect 6.1–6.2%; 2% experts expect above 6.2%. Overall, affected by COVID-19 pandemic, 95% experts believe that Chinese GDP growth rate in 2020 will be lower than the growth rate of 6.1% in 2019.

In 2019, Chinese CPI rose 2.9%, 0.8 percentage points higher than the previous year; the core CPI excluding food and energy rose 1.6%, 0.3 percentage points lower than the previous year. With regard to the growth rate of Chinese CPI in 2020, 44% experts expect it will be 2.9–3.3%; 33% experts expect 2.4–2.8%; 12% 3.4–3.8%; 9% experts expect below 2.3%; 2% experts expect above 3.9%. Overall, nearly 60% experts believe that the CPI in 2020 will be higher than in 2019.

In 2019, Chinese PPI decreased 0.3%, up 3.8 percentage points over the previous year. With regard to the growth rate of Chinese PPI in 2020, 40% experts expect it will be −1.0 to 0.0%; 38% experts expect 0–1.0%; 13% experts expect 1.0–2.0%; 8% experts expect −2.0 to 1.0%, and 1% experts expect above 2.0%. Overall, nearly 50% experts expect that in 2020 it will be lower than in 2019.

In 2019, Chinese fixed asset investment (excluding farmers) increased 5.4%, down 0.5 percentage points over the previous year. Among them, infrastructure investment grew 3.8%, as same as that of the previous year; manufacturing investment grew 3.1%, down 6.4 percentage points; real estate development investment grew 9.9%, up 0.4 percentage points. (1) With regard to the nominal growth rate of Chinese fixed asset investment in 2020, 51% experts expect it will be between 5.0–6.0%; 25% experts expect 4.0–5.0%; 13% experts expect 6.0–7.0%; 8% experts expect 3.0–4.0%; 3% experts expect above 7.0%. (2) With regard to the growth rate of Chinese manufacturing investment in 2020, 44% experts believe that it will continue to decline; 34% experts expect it will be basically the same as that in 2019; 22% experts expect believe it will accelerate. (3) With regard to the growth rate of real estate investment in 2020, 59% experts expect it will slow down; 33% experts believe that it will be basically unchanged; 8% experts expect it will accelerate. (4) With regard to infrastructure investment in 2020, 49% experts expect it will accelerate; 36% expect it will remain basically unchanged; 12% expect it will slow down; 3% expect it will accelerate, with an annual growth rate of about 4%.

To sum up, in 2020, More than 60% experts expect that the nominal growth rate of the fixed asset investment will be higher than 5.9% of 2019; more than 40% experts expect that the growth rate of manufacturing investment will slow down; nearly 60% experts expect that the growth rate of real estate investment will slow down; 60% experts expect that the growth rate of the real estate investment will decline. 50% experts expect that the growth rate of infrastructure investment will continue to accelerate.

In 2019, the investment of state-owned and state-holding enterprises increased 6.8%, up 4.9 percentage points over the previous year; private investment increased 4.7%, down 4 percentage points. (1) With regard to the investment of state-owned and state-holding enterprises in 2020, 69% experts believe that the growth rate will be 5.0–7.0%; 22% experts expect 7.0–9.0%; 7% experts expect below 5.0%; 1% experts expect 9.0–10.0%, and 1% experts expect above 10.0%. (2) With regard to the growth rate of private investment in 2020, 66% experts expect it will be 3.0–5.0%; 20% experts expect 7.0–9.0%; 11% experts expect below 3.0%; 3% experts expect 7.0–9.0%.

In 2019, Chinese total retail sales of consumer goods increased 8.0% in nominal terms (6.0% in real terms), and the growth rate was 1 percentage point lower than that of the previous year, and the retail sales of consumer goods excluding automobiles increased 9.0%. The survey show that 45% experts expect it will be 7.5–8.0%; 34% experts expect below 7.5%; 17% experts expect 8.0–8.5%; 3% experts expect 8.5–9.0%; 1% experts expect above 9.0%. Overall, 79% experts believe that the nominal growth rate of total retail sales of consumer goods in 2020 will be lower than the level of 2019, 8.0%.

In 2019, Chinese export of goods (in RMB) reached 17229.8 billion yuan, increasing 5.0% with a decline of 2.1 percentage points over the previous year. With regard to the growth rate of Chinese total exports (in RMB) in 2020, 42% experts expect it will be 4.0–5.0%; 35% experts expect below 4.0%; 17% experts expect 5.0–6.0%; 5% experts expect 6.0–7.0%; 1% experts expect above 7.0%. Overall, 77% experts believe that Chinese export growth rate in 2020 will be lower than the level of 2019, 5.0%.

In 2019, Chinese import of goods (in RMB) was 14314.8 billion yuan, increasing 1.6% with a decline of 11.3 percentage points over the previous year. With regard to growth rate of the total imports (in RMB) in 2020, 47% experts expect will be experts expect 0.0–2.0%; 37% experts expect 2.0–4.0%; 8% experts expect 4.0–6.0%; 4% experts expect below 0.0%; and 4% experts expect above 6.0%. Overall, more than 90% experts believe that the growth rate of imports will be higher than that in 2019.

Because China and the US reached the first phase of trade agreement, the exchange rate of RMB against the US dollar has shown a certain appreciation trend since December 2019. By the end of December 2019, the exchange rate was 6.976, decreasing 1.65% compared to the beginning of the year. Since 2020, the exchange rate has continued to appreciate. By January 20th, 2020, the exchange rate was 6.8664. The survey show that 36% experts expect the RMB will continue to depreciate against the US dollar, and the exchange rate at the end of 2020 is about 6.7–7.25, with an average value of 7.0124; 33% experts expect it will be basically stable in

2020; 31% experts expect that the RMB will appreciated, and in 2020 it will be about 6.6–7.05, with an average of 6.8523. Overall, 36% experts believe that the RMB will continue to depreciate against the US dollar in 2020.

Outlook for China's Macroeconomic Policy in 2020

By the end of December 2019, the balance of Chinese broad money (M2) was 198.65 trillion yuan, increasing 8.7%, an increase of 0.6 percentage points over the previous year. So, what will be the growth rate of M2 in China in 2020? 53% experts expect that the growth rate of M2 in China will be 8.7–9.2%; 30% experts expect 8.1–8.6%; 7% experts expect 9.3–9.8%; 5% experts expect below 8.1%; and 5% experts expect above 9.8%. Overall, 65% experts believe that Chinese M2 growth rate in 2020 will be higher than the level of 2019, 8.7%, indicating that most experts believe that the Chinese government will continue to adopt a prudent and neutral monetary policy in 2020.

According to the preliminary statistics of the People's Bank of China, the total social financing increased 25.58 trillion yuan, an increase of 3.08 trillion yuan over the previous year. Among them, the new RMB loans increased 16.88 trillion yuan; the new RMB loans accounted for 66% of the social financing scale in the same period, down 3.7 percentage points over the previous year. Among the new RMB loans in 2019, the loans to the real economy increased 9.45 trillion yuan, accounting for 56.2% of the total new loans, a sharp increase of 4.83 percentage points compared with 2018. So, what is the proportion of the new RMB loans to real economy in 2020? The survey results show that 68% experts expect it will be 55–60%; 14% experts expect 50–55%; 12% experts expect 60–65%; 4% experts expect above 65%; 2% experts expect below 50%.

The Central Economic Work Conference in 2019 proposed that: positive fiscal policies should improve quality and efficiency, pay more attention to structural adjustment, resolutely reduce general expenditures, do a good job in key areas, ensure wages, transport and basic people's livelihood; consolidate and expand the effect of taxes and fees cutting, and optimize the financial expenditure structure. So, what are the focus points of Chinese active fiscal policy in 2020? The survey show that 78% experts believe that "we should be committed to the reasonable growth of the economic and the steady improvement of the quality, so as to ensure the stable operation of the economy in a reasonable range"; 74% experts believe that "we should appropriately expand the deficit, especially the central fiscal deficit, to make room for taxes and fees cutting and increased expenditure to stabilize the infrastructure"; 68% experts believe that "through the rational allocation of financial funds, priority should be given to ensuring the improvement of people's livelihood and expenditure in key areas"; 63% experts believe that "the general government expenditure other than people's livelihood and social security should be reduced, the organization and personnel should be simplified, and the structure of financial expenditure should be optimized"; 63% experts believe that "both effective demand and structural adjustment should be expanded, and more attention should be paid to promoting structural adjustment"; 59% experts believe that "the way of taxes and fees cutting should be optimized. From the current perspective, it is mainly aimed at reducing the VAT, but China should give priority to reduce the social security rate and enterprise income tax rate"; 43% experts believe that "reform the financial system, give more power to local government, stabilize the half-half share of VAT between the central and local governments, and implement the consumption tax and gradually transfer it to local government". In addition, 10% experts put forward other different opinions, for example, China should further reduce the taxes and fees for the SMEs, give more financial support to prevent and control COVID-19 pandemic, improve financial support to implement the strategy of rural revitalization, build public projects, such as the construction of health and COVID-19 pandemic prevention system. The fiscal policies is taken precedence over monetary policies, which is expected to stabilize growth more, the monetary policies will more rely on new monetary policy tools; finance should support the establishment of some new state-owned enterprises, so that these new state-owned enterprises can play a greater role in stabilizing prices, ensuring people's lives and innovation; support key enterprises for COVID-19 pandemic prevention and control through financial subsidies and taxes cutting; expand the scale of infrastructure investment and consumer credit; and actively issue financial discount loans in response to the COVID-19 pandemic. During the COVID-19 pandemic period, taxes exemption, direct subsidy, interest subsidy, or the establishment of special anti-COVID-19 pandemic fund; specify the timing and form of property tax collection.

The Central Economic Working Conference in 2019 proposed that the prudent monetary policies should be flexible and appropriate, and the liquidity should be reasonable and abundant; the scale growth of monetary credit and social financing should adapt to the economic development, reduce the cost of social financing; increase the medium and long-term financing of the manufacturing industry, and alleviate the financing difficulties and expensive problems of the SMEs. So, what are the focus points of Chinese monetary policies in 2020? According to the survey results, 79% experts believe that "while maintaining reasonable and sufficient liquidity, China should focus on adjusting the structure of credit supply and significantly increase the proportion of new RMB loans to real economy"; 74% experts believe that "monetary policies emphasizes normal counter cyclical adjustment, not flooding with water, reducing interest rates through small, high frequency and reform, and reducing interest rates through cutting policy interest rate and other ways guide the real interest rate downward"; 68% experts believe that "continue to deepen the interest rate market-oriented reform, effectively promote the decline of the actual financing cost of enterprises"; 66% experts believe that "dredge the transmission mechanism of interest rate, improve liquidity stratification, eliminate ownership discrimination"; 59% experts believe that "monetary policies cannot be used alone, need to cooperate with other policies and form a joint force to keep the short-term demand balance and avoid economic ups and downs"; 57% experts believe that "we should implement the long-term mechanism for the stable and healthy development of the real estate market, rectify the over tight real estate financing, adhere to the principle of no speculation in real estate, stable land price, house price and expectation"; 48% experts believe that "we should stick to the stability of currency value, and at the same time, the Central Bank should also strengthen the goal of financial stability, and integrate the maintenance of currency value stability and financial stability". 8% experts put forward other different opinions, for example, special monetary policies for the prevention and controlling of COVID-19 pandemic, combined with post COVID-19 pandemic reconstruction, committed to structural complementarity, shifting from broad currency to wide credit, reducing the reserve ratio, and at least depreciating the RMB to about 7.2 against the US dollar; Deepen the reform of the financial system; strengthen the competition policy and anti-monopoly in the financial field; the monetary policies should be changed from prudent to active; issue targeted low interest loans to support the SMEs seriously affected by the COVID-19 pandemic, and ensure that the capital chain is not broken or no large-scale debt default occurs.

The judgment of the Central Economic Work Conference in 2019 on the current situation about "downward pressure is increasing on the economy", which is consistent with the statement of Political Bureau meeting 30th July. It emphasizes "downward pressure on the economy is increasing" and "Six Stability".[1] It is necessary to improve and strengthen the "Six Stability" measures, improve the coordination and transmission mechanism of fiscal, monetary, employment and other policies, and ensure that the economy operates within a reasonable range. The meeting "closely adheres to the goal and task of building a moderately prosperous society in an all respects", without mentioning leverage, which shows that China should put stable growth in a more prominent position. So, what are the policy measures to stabilize growth in 2020? The survey results show that 90% the experts believe that "actively develop advanced manufacturing industry, accelerate the transformation and upgrading of traditional manufacturing industry, and strengthen the construction of new infrastructure"; 82% experts believe that "giving priority to people's livelihood, narrowing the income inequality, increasing high-quality supply and transfer income, improving social security to promote consumption growth, increase effective investment and release the demand potential of domestic market"; 70% experts believe that "we should promote the stability and quality of foreign trade, guide enterprises to develop diversified export markets, reduce the general level of tariffs, release industry investment restrictions, strengthen the protection of intellectual property rights, and continuously improve the business environment"; 69% experts believe that "we should liberalize the market access of basic fields such as automobile, finance, energy, telecommunications, electricity and medical education and other service industries to cultivate the new economic growth points"; 63% experts believe that "deepen the reform of state-owned enterprises, implement competition neutrality and ownership neutrality, eliminate ownership discrimination, introduce market mechanism, and increase the vitality of enterprises and organizations"; 63% experts believe that "we should promote the marketization of interest rates, financial liberalization and serve the development of multi-level capital and financial market of

[1] "Six Stability" include: Stable employment, finance, foreign trade, foreign investment, domestic investment and expectation.

the real economy, and provide financing for emerging industries demand, promote the rapid rise of emerging industries"; 50% experts believe that "the Chinese government adds leverage, transfers leverage, reduce enterprises and residents burden, large-scale taxes and fees cutting, enhance vitality of the enterprises and residents". In addition, 8% experts put forward other views. For example, facing the economic impact of the COVID-19 pandemic, China should introduce relevant growth measures, take advantage of Chinese characteristics system, which can concentrate the whole country's power, win the battle against COVID-19 pandemic, increase the support to the collective enterprises of state-owned enterprises, and support the labor intensive firms and terminal consumer enterprises which affected by the COVID-19 pandemic by means of preferential tax and loan to reduce the impact of the COVID-19 pandemic on employment and consumption; strengthen the basic position of competition policy; boost infrastructure investment and open the real estate market; implement policies according to the actual situation of the city and relax the administrative control over the real estate industry; further expand the institutional opening in the free trade zone and free trade port, summarize the pilot experience.

"Stable employment" is the most important in "Six Stable" in 2019. In 2019, the absolute number of newly added urban employment was well completed, with 13.52 million new urban jobs, reaching 122.9% of the annual target. However, the employment of manufacturing industry and service industry reached lowest level in the past ten years, and "stable employment" will still be first priority of "Six Stable" in 2020. The 2019 Central Economic Work Conference emphasized "to stabilize the total employment, improve the employment structure, improve the quality of employment, focus on the employment of key groups of employees, and ensure the dynamic clearing of unemployed families". So, what are the policies and measures to stabilize employment in 2020? According to the survey 75% experts believe that "guiding the coordinated development of industrial transformation and employment promotion"; 73% believe that "implementing precise policies to do a good job in the employment of key groups of employees"; 72% experts believe that "further strengthening vocational skills training"; 67% experts believe that " expanding the openness to stabilize the growth of employment"; 67% believe that "more efforts to support entrepreneurship and innovation activities"; 58% experts believe that " building social safety net and give full play to improve unemployment insurance system"; 53% experts believe that " improving the early warning system of unemployment and eliminate the institutional obstacles of labor flow". 8% experts put forward other different opinions, such as: the steady employment measurements coping with impact COVID-19 pandemic; standardizing the layoff behavior of the enterprises; making full efforts to restore the economy after the COVID-19 pandemic prevention; making efforts to expand domestic demand, effectively improving the market environment for the SMEs; and implement policies according to the actual situation of the city, relaxing administrative control over the real estate industry. During the COVID-19 pandemic period, China should focus on supporting small and micro enterprises to stabilize employment; vigorously develop service industry, and increase the employment of low-skilled workers; and do a good job in stabilizing the unemployment of small and micro enterprises and creating new jobs after the COVID-19 pandemic.

The 2019 Central Economic Work Conference has specified the key tasks for 2020. So, what are the most prominent points? The survey show that 71% experts believe that "we should improve and strengthen the six stability measures, improve the coordination and transmission mechanism of fiscal, monetary, employment and other policies, and ensure that the economy operating within a reasonable range"; 66% experts believe that "we should resolutely fight three major battles to achieve the goal of building a moderately prosperous society in an all respects"; 61% experts believe that "ensuring people's livelihood, especially the basic life of the people in need, is effectively guaranteed and improved"; 61% experts believe that "efforts should be made to promote high-quality development"; 58% experts believe that "we should continue to implement active fiscal policy and prudent monetary policies"; 51% experts believe that "deepening economic system reform". In addition, 6% experts put forward other different views, such as: in the ownership structure, efforts should be made in the direction of increasing the proportion of the public sector of the economy; improving the ability of national governance to adapt to economic reform and development; improving the financial system of division of labor and cooperation, improving classified supervision and disposal policies for different types of financial institutions; strengthening the basic position of competition policies; During the COVID-19 pandemic period, China should focus on supporting small and micro enterprises to stabilize employment, narrow the income inequality, increase employment opportunities, and improve the income level of residents. The first task is to do a good job in the control of the COVID-19 pandemic, and vigorously do a good job in economic recovery after the COVID-19 pandemic.

A.2 Questionnaire Survey II

March 18th–25th, 2020

On March 16, 2020, the National Bureau of Statistics published economic data for January and February. The data showed that "COVID-19 pandemic has affected greatly to the economic operation. But overall, the impact of the COVID-19 pandemic is short and controllable." For this reason, we have specially organized the second stage of questionnaire survey. The questionnaire designed 21 questions directly related to the COVID-19 pandemic impact, macroeconomic trends and policies in 2020. In March 2020, the questionnaire sent an invitation to China domestic economists by email, and finally received a response from 105 experts. The results of this questionnaire are published as follows.

Impact of COVID-19 Pandemic on China's Economy

According to the preliminary accounting data released by the National Bureau of statistics on January 17, 2020, Chinese GDP grew 6.1% in 2019, down 0.5% over the previous year. On March 16, 2020, the National Bureau of Statistics published economic data for January and February. The data indicate that COVID-19 pandemic has affected greatly on the economy. With regard to Chinese GDP growth rate in 2020, the survey show that 34% experts expect it will be 5.0–5.5%; 25% experts expect 4.5–5.0%; 25% experts expect 4.0–4.5%; 14% experts expect 5.5–6.0%; and 2% experts expect above 6.0%. Overall, almost all experts believe that the GDP growth rate in China will be less than 6% in 2020. 50% of experts believe that the growth rate of Chinese GDP will be less than 5% in 2020.

With regard to the growth rate of Chinese GDP in the first quarter of 2020, the survey show that 49% experts expect it will be −4.0 to −1.0%; 26% experts expect −1.0 to 1.0%; 18% experts expect 1.0–3.0%; 7% experts expect 3.0–5.0%. In general, 75% experts believe that the growth rate of Chinese GDP in the first quarter of 2020 will be less than 1%, and nearly 50% experts believe that the growth rate will be negative.

In 2019, Chinese fixed asset investment (excluding farmers) increased 5.4%, down 0.5 percentage points over the previous year. Affected by the COVID-19 pandemic, the growth rate of fixed asset investment (excluding households) in January and February 2020 was down 24.5% compared with the previous year. Among them, infrastructure investment fell 30.3%, manufacturing investment fell 31.5%, and real estate investment fell 16.3%. So, what is the growth rate of the fixed asset investment in 2020? The survey show that 32% experts expect it will be 5.0–6.0%; 23% experts expect 4.0–5.0%; 23% experts expect 6.0–7.0%; 11% experts expect 7.0–8.0%; 11% experts expect above 8.0%. Overall, over 75% experts believe that the growth rate of Chinese fixed asset investment in 2020 will be higher than that in 2019.

In 2019, Chinese total retail sales of social consumption goods increased 8.0% in nominal terms (6.0% in real terms, excluding price factors), and the growth rate was 1.0 percentage point lower than that of the previous year. Affected by the COVID-19 pandemic, the total retail sales of consumer goods decreased 20.5% in January and February in 2020. The growth rate of retail sales online in China fell 3.0%. Among them, the online retail sales of physical goods reached 1123.3 billion yuan, an increase of 3.0%, accounting for 21.5% of the total retail sales of consumer goods, up 5.0 percentage points over the same period last year. So, what will be the growth rate of total retail sales of consumer goods in China in 2020? According to the survey, 40% experts expect it will be 6.0–7.0%; 37% experts expect 5.0–6.0%; 16% experts expect 7.0–8.0%; 6% experts expect 8.0–9.0%; 1.0% experts expect above 9.0%. Overall, 93% experts believe that it will be lower than the level of 2019, 8.0%.

In 2019, Chinese CPI rose 2.9%, 0.8 percentage points higher than the previous year. Affected by the COVID-19 pandemic, CPI rose 5.3% in January and February in 2020, and the core CPI excluding food and energy rose 1.3%. Consumer prices rose 5.4 and 5.2% over the previous year in January and February, respectively. With regard to the change trend of Chinese CPI in 2020, 33% experts expect it will be 3.0–3.5%; 28% experts expect 3.5–4.0%; 16% experts expect above 4.0%; 15% experts expect 2.0–3.0%; 8% experts expect 1.0–2.0%. Overall, 77% experts believe that Chinese annual CPI growth in 2020 will be higher than the level of 2019, 2.9%.

In 2019, Chinese PPI decreased 0.3%, up 3.8 percentage points over the previous year. Affected by the COVID-19 pandemic, the PPI rose 0.1% and fell 0.4% in January and February respectively, compared with the previous year. With regard to the change trend of Chinese PPI in 2020, 44% experts expect it will be −1.0 to 1.0%; 26% experts expect 1.0–3.0%; 22% experts expect −3.0 to −1.0%; 5% experts expect −4.0 to −3.0%; 3% experts expect above 3.0%. Overall, more than 70% experts expect that Chinese PPI growth will be less than 1.0% in 2020, and there is still a large possibility of negative growth.

In 2019, Chinese foreign investment reached 941.52 billion yuan. Affected by the COVID-19 pandemic, what is the possible range of Chinese FDI growth in 2020? According to the survey, 38% experts expect it will be 0.0–3.0%; 22% experts expect below −3.0%; 20% experts expect 3.0–6.0%; 17% experts expect −3.0 to 0.0%; 3% experts expect above 6.0%. Overall, most experts believe that the growth rate of Chinese FDI in 2020 will be lower than that in 2019, and nearly 40% experts believe that there will be negative growth in 2020.

Affected by the COVID-19 pandemic, what is the growth rate of local government debt in 2020? The survey show that 47% experts expect it will be 15.0–30.0%; 30% experts expect 30.0–45.0%; 11% experts expect 45.0–60.0%; 11% experts expect 0.0–15.0%; 1.0% experts expect above 60.0%.

In 2018 and 2019, Chinese fiscal deficit rate was 2.6 and 2.8% respectively. Affected by the COVID-19 pandemic, what is the deficit rate to GDP in 2020? The survey results show that 35% experts expect it will be 3.3%; 33% experts expect 3.0–3.3%; 19% experts expect above 3.6%; 12% experts expect 2.7–3.0%; 1.0% experts expect 2.4–2.7%. In general, almost all experts believe that Chinese fiscal deficit rate in 2020 will be higher than that in 2019, and nearly 90% experts believe that it will be higher than the international warning line of 3%.

At the end of 2019, the registered urban unemployment rate of the whole country is 3.62%. Affected by the COVID-19 pandemic, what is the trend of urban unemployment rate in China in 2020? The survey show that 31% experts expect it will be 4.1–4.3%; 28% experts expect above 4.3%; 25% experts expect 3.9–4.1%; 15% experts expect 3.7–3.9%; 1.0% experts expect 3.5–3.7%. In general, almost all experts believe that the urban unemployment rate in 2020 will be higher than that in 2019.

In 2019, the per capita disposable income of Chinese residents was 30,733 yuan, an increase of 5.8% over the previous year. Affected by the COVID-19 pandemic, what is the growth rate of per capita disposable income in China in 2020? The survey show that 39% experts expect it will be 2.0–4.0%; 31% experts expect 0.0–2.0%; 16% experts expect 4.0–6.0%; 13% experts expect −2.0 to 0.0%; 1.0% experts expect above 6.0%. In general, almost all experts expect that the growth rate of per capita disposable income in China in 2020 will be lower than that in 2019.

Affected by the COVID-19 pandemic, what is the trend of the capacity utilization rate (assuming 100% in the same period last year) of enterprises in the first quarter of 2020? The survey show that 42% experts expect it will be 50.0–60.0%; 35% experts expect 60.0–70.0%; 12% experts expect below 50.0%; 11% experts expect 70.0–80.0%. In general, all experts believe that the capacity utilization rate of enterprises in the first quarter of 2020 is lower than 80%.

Affected by the COVID-19 pandemic, what is the trend of the capacity utilization rate (assuming 100% in the same period last year) of enterprises in the second quarter of 2020? The survey show that 32% experts expect it will be experts expect 75.0–80.0%; 27% experts expect 80.0–85.0%; 21% experts expect 85.0–90.0%; 10% experts expect 90.0–95.0%; and 10% experts expect above 95.0%. Overall, 90% experts believe that the capacity utilization rate of enterprises in the second quarter of 2020 will be lower than that of the same period last year, and nearly 70% of experts believe that it will be higher than 80%.

Affected by the COVID-19 pandemic, what is the trend of enterprise bankruptcy rate in 2020? The survey results show that 40% experts expect it will be 3.0–6.0%; 35% experts expect 6.0–9.0%; 19% experts expect 9.0–12.0%; 4% experts expect 0.0–3.0%; 2% experts expect above 12.0%.

Outlook for China's Macroeconomic Policy in 2020

Affected by the COVID-19 pandemic, what is the biggest threat to Chinese financial system risk in 2020? In 2017, 2018 and 2019, the non-performing loan (NPL or bad loan) ratio of Chinese commercial banks was 1.74, 1.89 and 1.86%, respectively. What is the trend of the NPL ratio of Chinese commercial banks in 2020? According to the survey, 29% experts expect it will be 2.05–2.20%; 27% experts expect 1.90–2.05%; 27% experts expect 2.20–2.35%; 12% experts expect above 2.35%; 5% experts expect 1.75–1.90%. In general, more than 90% experts believe that the NPL ratio of Chinese commercial banks in 2020 will be higher than that in the past three years.

In 2018 and 2019, the price of new housing rose by 10.7 and 6.5% respectively. Affected by the COVID-19 pandemic, what will be the growth rate of the price of new housing in 2020? The survey show that 53% experts expect it will be 0.0–4.0%; 23% experts expect 4.0–8.0%; 18% experts expect −4.0 to 0.0%; 5% experts expect above 8.0%; 1.0% experts expect below −4.0%. Overall, more than 70% experts believe that the growth rate of price of housing in 2020 will be lower than that in 2019.

Affected by COVID-19 pandemic, what is the trend of stock market (Shanghai Stock Index) in 2020? According to the survey, 38% experts expect it will rise 0–10%; 32% experts expect −10 to 0%; 14% experts expect above 10%; 13% experts expect −20 to −10%; 3% experts expect below −20%. Overall, nearly half of the experts believe that Chinese stock market will show a downward trend in 2020.

With regard to the biggest threat to Chinese financial systemic risk in 2020, according to the survey, 49% experts think it is "the failure of the SMEs, and the increase in unemployment"; 18% experts think it is "the increase in local government debt"; 13% experts think it is "the rise of non-performing loan rate of banks"; 8% experts think it is "the fall of asset price"; 4% of the experts think it is "the lack of consumption demand"; 4% experts think it is "the strength of fiscal and monetary policy is less than expected"; 2% experts think it is "rising inflation"; 2% experts think it is "industrial supply chain transfer". In general, nearly half of the experts believe that the biggest threat to Chinese financial systemic risk in 2020 will be "the collapse of the SMEs and the rise of unemployment rate".

In order to cope with the impact of the COVID-19 pandemic, what are the most urgent policy measures for the SMEs? According to the survey, experts believe that the most urgent policy measures for the SMEs are as follows: First, make more efforts to cut taxes and fees, accelerate the implementation of phased and targeted taxes and fees cutting measures, and increase the taxes refund and concessions for industries and enterprises that are more affected by the COVID-19 pandemic; Second, increase the support for enterprises which stabilize the employment, provide subsidies, solve the shortage problems of labor and raw materials, build an online and offline service platform for human resources, provide free recruitment and agency services for enterprises, encourage human resources service institutions to provide recruitment services for enterprises, give certain subsidies to institutions, boost the resumption of work, production, and business activities; Third, reduce the burden of enterprises. Enterprises should be allowed to postpone the payment of tax, to postpone the payment of social insurance premium or housing fund, postpone the VAT of small enterprises, and reduce the rent. In terms of the tax reduction and exemption of the SMEs, if it is really difficult to pay the real estate tax and urban land use tax, it is possible to apply for the reduction and exemption of the real estate tax and urban land use tax; Fourth, financial support for the SMEs should be increased, which greatly affected by the COVID-19 pandemic situation; Fifth, reduce the financing cost of the SMEs, appropriately extend the maturity debt, provide low interest rate loans; Sixth, provide the SMEs with necessary free liquidity financial support, provide enterprises with financial more services and support; Seventh, treat large and medium-sized enterprises and enterprises with different ownership equally and implement the principle of competition neutrality; Eighth, improve the business environment of the SMEs; Ninth, guide the SMEs to adapt to the industrial restructuring after the COVID-19 pandemic; Tenth, set up special rescue funds to improve the financial availability of the SMEs and play the role of special funds.

In order to reduce the impact of the COVID-19 pandemic, should the focus of Chinese monetary policy be adjusted in 2020? What are the key areas of adjustment? According to the survey results, 92% experts believe that the focus of Chinese monetary policies in 2020 should be adjusted. The key areas of adjustment include: First, reduce the reserve and interest rate, reduce the reserve ratio of financial institutions, reduce the open market interest rate, the medium-term lending (MLF) interest rate, the loan prime rate (LPR), and the interest rate of enterprises, especially financing cost of the SMEs, provide short-term and medium-term liquidity; Second, maintain reasonable and sufficient liquidity of the banking system, and continue to promote the LPR reform; Third, the monetary policies should emphasize stable growth, appropriately ease the monetary policy, strengthen the support for manufacturing industry, especially high-tech industry, and focus on the real economy; Fourth, actively guide the market interest rate downward, and effectively reduce the financing cost of the real economy, strengthen the support for the affected areas and industries, especially for the regional financial differential policies such as the key support for Hubei Province; Fifth, increase the counter cyclical adjustment, focus on guiding market expectations, and increase the structural loans and preferential loans to SMEs; Sixth, increase the targeted easing and give play to the role of directional guidance, to promote the directional flow of financial elements; Seventh, speed up the improvement of the way in which the basic currency is put into use; Eighth, maintain a loose situation, implement special credit support policies, and ensure that the financing needs of the real economy are fully met; Ninth, the Central Bank should bypass the commercial banking system and directly invest in the basic strategic assets to put money into the market; Tenth, continue to increase special refinancing and the amount of refinancing rediscount, work with China Banking and Insurance Regulatory Commission and other departments to extend and renewal to the SMEs and private enterprises that have been greatly affected by the COVID-19 pandemic, so as to help these enterprises maintain the stability of cash flow and overcome difficulties. In addition, 8% experts believe that the focus of Chinese monetary policies in 2020 does not need to be adjusted.

In order to reduce the impact of the COVID-19 pandemic, should the focus of Chinese fiscal policy be adjusted in 2020? What are the key areas of adjustment? According to the survey, 96% experts believe that the focus of Chinese fiscal policy in 2020 should be adjusted. The key areas include: First, increase investment in "new infrastructure" and strengthen investment plans for "new infrastructure", including increasing investment in social infrastructure, urban and rural public medical facilities, elderly care facilities and urban infrastructure construction in metropolitan areas; Second, more efforts should be made to cut taxes and fees, reduce or delay the implementation of relevant taxes, and increase the support of financial funds to private enterprises, especially the SMEs. Third, China should appropriately increase the financial deficit rate, expand the scale of the central budget deficit and the scale of local government debt issuance. Fourth, China should expand the special debt model, relax the limit of local debt, issue more local bonds and government bonds, and consider issuing special government bonds, China should issue long-term construction bonds to boost infrastructure investment. Fifth, China should increase financial subsidies to industries that have been hit hard by the COVID-19 pandemic. China should provide targeted support through various ways to regions and industries that have been affected by the COVID-19 pandemic. Targeted subsidies will support enterprises to resume production, expand effective investment demand, and promote the upgrading of consumption structure. Sixth, China should reduce administrative costs and expand the public sector, optimize the structure of fiscal expenditure, pay more attention to structural adjustment, and ensure that the key areas include social expenditure, at the same time, increase public investment; Seventh, China should reduce the tax rates of enterprises and individuals at different stages, and further reduce the personal income tax of middle and low-income residents; Eighth, China should purchase corporate bonds equity and so on. In addition, 4% experts believe that the focus of Chinese fiscal policy in 2020 does not need to be adjusted.

Appendix B
Forecast of Major Indicators of China's Economy in 2020 by the CQMM Team and Experts

Major indicators in 2020	By CQMM team (%)	By experts before COVID-19 (%)		By experts after COVID-19 (%)	
		Interval	Ratio	Interval	Ratio
GDP	4.59 to 5.09	5.9 5.9 to 6.0	63 24	5.0 to 5.5 4.5 to 5.0 4.0 to 4.5	34 25 25
GDP in the Q1	−3.81 to 0.94			−4.0 to −1.0 −1.0 to 1.0 1.0 to 3.0	49 26 18
Fixed asset investment (excluding farmers)	6.60 to 8.13	5.0 to 6.0	51	5.0 to 6.0 4.0 to 5.0 6.0 to 7.0	32 23 23
Nominal total retail sales	5.79 to 7.58	7.5 to 8.0 7.5以下 8.0 to 8.5	45 34 17	6.0 to 7.0 5.0 to 6.0 7.0 to 8.0	40 37 16
CPI	3.21 to 3.27	2.9 to 3.3 2.4 to 2.8	44 33	3.0 to 3.5 3.5 to 4.0 up to 4.0	33 28 16
PPI	−3.25 to −3.54	−1.0 to 0.0 0.0 to 1.0	40 38	−1.0 to 1.0 1.0 to 3.0 −3.0 to −1.0	44 26 22

China's Macroeconomic Outlook, Current Chinese Economic Report Series,
https://doi.org/10.1007/978-981-15-9279-9

The manufacturer's authorised representative in the EU is Springer Nature Customer Service Centre GmbH, Europaplatz 3, 69115 Heidelberg, Germany. If you have any concerns regarding our products, please contact ProductSafety@springernature.com

Printed and bound by CPI Group (UK) Ltd, Croydon, CR0 4YY
30/09/2026
02225470-0005